Caulfield, Shiela #911-NYPD

JOHN CAULFIELD

Caulfield, Shield #911-NYPD

JOHN CAULFIELD

Published by The Shield #911-NYPD Foundation, Inc.

www.CaulfieldShield911.org

iUniverse, Inc.
Bloomington

Caulfield, Shield #911-NYPD

iUniverse books may be ordered through booksellers or by contacting:

iUniverse
1663 Liberty Drive
Bloomington, IN 47403
www.iuniverse.com
1-800-Authors (1-800-288-4677)

Because of the dynamic nature of the Internet, any web addresses or links contained in this book may have changed since publication and may no longer be valid. The views expressed in this work are solely those of the author and do not necessarily reflect the views of the publisher, and the publisher hereby disclaims any responsibility for them.

Any people depicted in stock imagery provided by Thinkstock are models, and such images are being used for illustrative purposes only.

Certain stock imagery © Thinkstock.

ISBN: 978-1-4697-9979-7 (sc)
ISBN: 978-1-4697-9981-0 (hc)
ISBN: 978-1-4697-9980-3 (e)

Printed in the United States of America

iUniverse rev. date: 4/13/2012

Table of Contents

Chapter 1: Da Bronx! (And beyond)

I was born on March 12, 1929, six months prior to the Great Depression, in the South Bronx. My father, John, was an Irish immigrant from the town of Carrickmacross, County Monaghan, Ireland. He arrived in New York with his brother, Mike, not long after the Irish Rebellion in Dublin. My mother, Marian nee Martin, was also born in the Bronx of Irish immigrant parents.

At that time, Irish kids in the Bronx either grew up to be firemen, cops, or priests. And so from a young age, I knew that my future held one of these three options. However, the path I took into law enforcement wasn't exactly direct.

I remember my father telling me as a child about the Black and Tans, the British-supported constabulary that ruled Ireland in the 1920s when he was a teen. The nickname name came from the khaki and dark uniforms they wore. He said that when they came to town, the children ran for cover, owing to the penchant of the Tans to inflict summary punishment on any who failed to immediately obey their arbitrary laws.

Most accounts described them as undisciplined former British soldiers, happy to earn "Soldier of Fortune" money at the expense of the Irish population. So, the hope and wish for Irish freedom was deep-seated in my relatives.

Regis Philbin, a Bronx Irish Catholic like me, recently informed his TV audience that the Bronx's first settler was a Dutchman named Jonas Bronk, who arrived here in the early part of the seventeenth century. Somehow his large property holding became anglicized to "The Bronx," or, if you were born there in modern times, bearing a heavy "Nu Yauk" accent, "Da Bronx."

1

My folks, when first married, took a Bronx apartment adjacent to 138th Street and Alexander Avenue. On the southeast corner was St. Jerome's Catholic Church. On the northeast corner, appropriately, was a well-trafficked Irish saloon. And, on the northwest corner was the 40th Police Precinct, inevitably busy, with Saturday night visitors.

So, if one behaved himself, went to Mass, and didn't get too drunk, he could avoid a night in the slammer across the street. Many went to Mass alright, but more than a few failed at the other two options. Such was life for many south Bronx Irish at that time.

Near my folk's apartment was the Innisveil Ballroom, where many Irish celebrated marriage and went dancing on Saturday night. My mom and dad met at that location. I recall my father's humorous description of a few fights that he was involved in there. While no John L. Sullivan, he must have been pretty good, in that he earned the nickname "John the Bull."

Like so many other Bronx families of the Depression, life for us was a struggle. My father, with only a minimal education, was constantly scrambling for any type of work. I recall watching him in the brutal heat of August one day, chopping eighty-pound blocks of ice in the street and delivering them on his shoulder to the tenants' ice boxes. He also worked at the zoo, cleaning out animal cages.

His first job in New York was working with immigrant Italians digging road ditches. I asked him one day about the type of benefits he receive from that job. He gave an answer I haven't forgot: "Well, Johnny, those that worked the hardest got paid first, my brother Mike and I always were the furst paid," (not exactly a 401K!). Eventually, he found good work with the New York Telephone Company, from whence he retired.

My first job, at age ten, was working before and after school in a small grocery store owned by a Jewish merchant. I packed shelves, delivered customers' orders, and on Jewish high holy days made ten cents for turning the Jewish tenants' stoves on. My weekly salary was two American dollars, which I proudly gave to my mom. I guess one could say that that was a real minimum wage.

I went to St. Martin of Tours grammar school taught by the Dominican nuns, who did a heck of a job. The parish was primarily comprised of Sicilian and Irish residents. Although some won't believe it, I became an

Altar Boy, and learned the Latin phrases I would need to participate with the priest at Mass. It was an interesting experience.

I sure wasn't the smartest kid in the class of 1943, but I did spell well enough to get entered in a grammar school spelling contest. I didn't win, but looking back, the die had been cast: Irish words, rather than Jewish math, were where I was headed.

I often found myself in the local library, devouring bestsellers like *The Call of the Wild* and *Guadalcanal Diary*. Resultantly, I agree with those who see the merits of early reading, possibly before all else, in the education of the child.

One of my schoolboy friends, Joe Vito, brought me to his apartment house one evening and as we entered the vestibule I was startled by the pungent odor of Italian cooking coming from just about every apartment in the building. His mom gave me my first taste of pizza that night, and like so many of us, I became addicted ever since.

The immigrant and first generation New York Irish found their dream weekend retreat at Rockaway Beach on the Atlantic in Queens, New York. In one mile and a half stretch, adjacent or close to the ocean, there were about fifty bars, saloons, and dance halls. The crowd often exceeded 25,000 on a Saturday night. Recently, I learned that the name Rockaway is derived from a seventeenth century Native American tribe called "Rockaways," who apparently inhabited that part of Queens.

My folks rented a bungalow there in the summer of 1941 when I was just twelve. I delivered early-edition newspapers to those bars and dance halls, starting around 9:00 p.m. It was there I first experienced the foot-tapping joy of listening to the rebel and other classic Irish songs, while watching the wildly happy dancers going full bore at their jigs and reels; perhaps not too unlike the Rockaways dancers?

In any event, the spectacle was like a continuous weekend St. Patrick's Day party. And I quickly learned that I sold more newspapers and got bigger tips at midnight than at nine; one might call it the "supply and booze" syndrome or, if you like, "the later bird catches the drunk."

Speaking of Rockaway and alcohol (some cynical friends call it "Irish heroin"); I had my first drink experience there at age fifteen with friends on the moon-lit beach. I proceeded to down straight shots of Southern Comfort, where upon I threw up, blacked out, and later told others what a great time I had. Little did I realize that I had taken my first fateful step towards becoming afflicted with alcoholism?

Recently, I asked myself, "What was the best Christmas gift I ever got?" Without a doubt, it was the basketball I received when I was ten years old. Not having access to a net, I improvised by shooting it through the bottom rung of the fire escape ladders, located on every tenement building. I sure had plenty of "courts" to practice on. I don't think that even James Naismith, the Canadian-born inventor of basketball who used peach baskets as the forerunner of today's netting, could have envisioned that innovation!

I remember becoming fascinated with the game when they put up crude nets on a wooden backboard, in the school's auditorium. I made a softball-sized basketball from paper and spent hours shooting alone in my privately created basketball world. At about that time, I was allowed to go and see my first basketball game played by the parish "Big Five." I came away forever hooked on the game, thereafter practically living on the neighborhood basketball court.

I attended Rice High School, run by the capable order of Irish Christian Brothers, in Harlem. I made the varsity team coached by the colorful, Tom Gorman. He was famed for winning the Catholic High School basketball championship for Power Memorial High School in the final seconds by making an incredible tip-in from a jump ball at the foul line! I have never heard of anyone ever doing that in a game, anywhere.

Power was also run by the Irish Christian Brothers. Lew Alcindor, son of a law enforcement officer, was also a Power basketball player. He led them to three consecutive CHSAA championships, along with a seventy-two-game winning streak.

After taking the Muslim name, Kareem Abdul Jabbar, the seven-foot, two-inch giant became one of the country's best all-time players with the Los Angeles Lakers in the NBA. He was raised a Catholic, but converted to Islam later on when he discovered he had family roots dating to the Jamaican slave trade.

Recently, in a TV interview about his new book, *On the Shoulders of Giants*, he mentioned that as he exited the 125th Street subway station, he found himself right in the middle of the Harlem Riot of July 1964; and witnessed, firsthand, the madness of Molotov cocktails being thrown from tenant windows.

Coincidentally, I did too as an NYPD detective, investigating the cause of that riot. Turned out we had a black undercover detective planted in a violence-prone Black Nationalist group, which was, quite effectively, inciting the riot by distributing to Harlem youths instructional pamphlets on how to make and use Molotov cocktails.

At the height of the deteriorating riot, the detective bosses decided to put a recording device on the detective and send him in to the group's headquarters (located only one block from Rice High School! My alma mater!) to get incriminating admissions—a dangerous assignment to say the least.

My black detective partner, Eddie Lee, and I were told to put on our patrolman's uniforms and station ourselves in front of the headquarters, functioning as a backup in the event anything went sour. If it did, the undercover detective was to throw a chair through the office window and we were to go in and get him out.

It was a long, tension-filled hour for us, worrying about the safety of our brother officer upstairs, with Molotov cocktails landing close by. But the detective pulled it off without a hitch—got the goods on the inciters, allowing for their summary arrest, and, thankfully, a rapid end to the riot. It was a commendable job, and he way properly promoted to detective by the NYPD Commissioner.

Before coaching at Rice, Gorman was a baseball pitcher in the Majors, jumping to the Mexican League, when that became economically fashionable. After leaving his Rice duties, he became a leading Major League umpire who once received quite a bit of notoriety. When working behind the plate, a foul tip from a Jackie Robinson's bat slammed into his unprotected throat, sending him to the hospital. The incident caused a much-needed improvement in catcher/umpire mask technology. Interestingly, his son also became a Major League umpire, and still is at this writing.

My basketball play at Rice improved in my senior year to the point where I was averaging about thirteen points per game. I was getting a big head, until one night I got a pretty good wakeup call about the tenuous realities of my two-handed set shot. We had a big-deal night game coming up at a large National Guard regiment armory in Manhattan. Most of our games were played in humble high school gyms, including Rice's.

So, at about 2:00 p.m. on the day of the game, I decided to go to the local YMCA and take practice set shots alone for an hour or so. I was amazed to find myself in a shooting zone few athletes ever experience. I literally couldn't miss from any location on the floor! I kept looking around for someone to witness what was happening, but no one was around.

I thought if I could do anything close to that in the upcoming game, I was sure to have at least a career scoring night. During the game's warm-ups, the zone continued. Spectators and teammates began to pay attention. Coach Gorman, also seeing this, called me over and said, "I want you to do a lot of shooting tonight, Jack."

I said, "Right, coach!" The first time I got my hand on the ball, I was way outside the top of the key, I let it go . . . swish, nothing but net! I said to myself, "Holy ------!"

Then I took twelve more set shots . . . and not one went in! My "Twilight Zone" moment was gone, never to return.

A great high school experience was the annual march up Fifth Avenue on St. Patrick's Day. We trained for the event in front of curious Harlem onlookers down the block from Rice High School. The parade ended on East 86th Street, the German section of Yorkville. It was a wonderful place to celebrate by getting drunk with just about every other Irishman in New York.

In any event, via the help of Gorman, I received a scholarship to, of all places, Wake Forest College in North Carolina. It was then a small Baptist college, located about fifteen miles north of Raleigh. Later, the school received a large grant from the Reynolds Tobacco Company, and then became a university, relocating to Winston Salem.

When I arrived by train for my tryout in August of 1947, it was only my second time outside of New York. The first was a memorable auto trip to Scranton, Pennsylvania, for a Labor Day weekend visit with my father and his friends. Indoor plumbing had not yet arrived there, so I had my first and only outhouse experience. As we left Scranton's main street on September 1, 1939, I was amazed to see newsboys running through the street yelling, "Get it here! Get it here! War in Europe! War in Europe!" The Nazis had invaded Poland.

The coach was not at the Wake Forest train station when I arrived, so I headed into the two-block town to call him. As I was walking towards a public phone, an elderly black man exited the sidewalk when we were about to pass one another. Huh? What was that about? Seconds later another black man did the same thing, just as I saw the shocking sign over a not-so-public water fountain that read, "WHITES ONLY." The stain of racial prejudice was alive and well in that part of North Carolina.

My thoughts went back to how I went home from basketball practice at Rice. It required a four-block walk, passing Harlem tenements, on the way to the 3rd Avenue El Station. I developed the necessary habit of walking in the middle of the street, because it was not unusual for missiles to be hurled at white passersby, or for black male tenants to emit threatening words, punctuated especially by two memorable ones, and they were not "Merry Christmas!" So, there was a Harlem culture, a Deep South Culture . . . and never the twain did meet at those times and places.

The one and only, Arnold Palmer, was a classmate of mine at Wake Forest, along with his golf teammate, Buddy Worsham. Buddy and I became close friends. His brother, Lew, won the U.S. Open Golf Championship, beating the great Sam Snead, to deny him the only major title he failed to achieve.

Just prior to the end of his junior year, Buddy was tragically killed in an auto accident en route to a party at Duke University in Durham, North Carolina; Arnold had been invited too, but fortuitously decided to pass. He was so shaken by Buddy's death that he dropped out of school. But he went on to win the U.S. Amateur Championship, turned pro, and the rest is memorable golf history. To his credit, he later formed the Worsham Memorial Fund, which still exists to this day.

One day, when he was at his professional peak, I took my three sons to see him play at the Westchester Country Club in New York. When he was warming up, he spotted me because I was wearing my Wake Forest basketball sweater, bearing a big gold W. He waved and told me to meet him after he finished. Gratuitously, he then gave my three sons and ad-hoc putting lesson, which neither one of them (nor I) would forget.

I had not only become hooked on golf at the relatively late age of twenty-five, but passed the addition on to my three sons. All three were on the same Robinson High School, golf and basketball teams, which, to say the least, got me back into the habit of biting my nails. Chris, who was runner-up in the Metropolitan New York Collegiate Championship when he was a senior at Manhattan College, has been a PGA professional for twenty-five years.

He has won his share of pro tournaments, including a mini-major at a PGA National course in West Palm Beach, competing against 125 other club pros from around the country. This year he is eligible for the Champions Tour and is going to give it the "ole college try." If he makes it, I will have nubs for fingers! My two other sons, John and Rich (Chris's twin) play at scratch, and are darn good amateur champions, each having won their share of amateur events.

So, my college basketball career began, but it turned out to be short lived. I had worked with a passion in the pre-season practice sessions and was delighted to find myself on the starting five, as the season opener approached. Pretty good, I thought, for an eighteen-year-old freshman competing against WWII vets.

But, Murphy's Law took over. I had my first cigarette at age twelve on a tenement rooftop, where I also had a newspaper route. By the time I got to Wake Forest, I had become a pack-a-day man. Realizing that my endurance would be affected if I continued, I managed to get it down to one a day, to be enjoyed after practice.

As I emerged from practice one evening, I lit up at the precise moment the coach, Murray Greason, was passing by in his auto. To my amazement, I instantly became an outcast, with "my sin" and punishment, announced to all team members. Horrors! The season opener was but weeks away and I was unceremoniously barred from participation during early season play. Huh!

Actually, I was not that unhappy in that I got to go home for Christmas, instead of having to remain at school for practice. I also enjoyed jumping around in the ten-foot-high snow drifts caused by the second greatest blizzard (1947) in the history of the City.

Thus began a downhill relationship between me and the coach. I did enjoy the road trips, however, and my limited playing time against some of the more formidable opponents like, NC State and North Carolina. When we played against Duke, our students jokingly sang and shouted, "Don't give a damn for Duke University . . . cause I'm from Wake Forest!"

One night in a game against Pittsburgh University, I got a memorable lesson. They had a six-foot-nine black center who became an All-American, the first of his race to accomplish that. I frequently took my two-handed set shots from the top of the key, where opposition defense was usually slack. As soon as I let one go that night, I knew it was in . . . until that player came from nowhere and slammed the ball down the other end of the court. I stood with my mouth wide open in amazement.

We went to play LaSalle University at a big public arena in Philadelphia—big-time stuff. I asked my folks to drive down to see the game. They had never seen me play in a basketball game. I went to the coach, told him my parents were coming down from New York, and respectfully asked him to get me into the game, even if it was only for a couple of minutes. He looked right through me, ignoring my request. I decided that night that my college basketball career was over. I hope that I became wiser as a result of that traumatic experience.

Returning to New York, I decided it was time to fulfill a longtime desire, to become an NYPD cop. I took and passed the mental and physical exams, and was anxiously waiting to be called. But Uncle Sam had the one-up call. I was to have a different title: Private First Class. It wasn't that bad though, when I was ordered to take basic training at nearby, Fort Monmouth, New Jersey; close enough so I could get home on weekends.

One fellow draftee was Whitely Ford, the 1950 World Series MVP. They gave him a brand new Pontiac. Whitey, always cagy, knew that he drank a bit too much occasionally, so he asked if I would meet him at Grand Central Station on Sunday nights and drive him back to camp. No problem.

One day he asked me to catch for him outside our barracks because he wanted to maintain his pitching skills. I belatedly realized that I should have had additional protection for my soon-to-be-swelling left hand. His pitching speed and accuracy were truly awesome.

I decided the best way for me to spend my two-year draft commitment was to join the Post basketball team. The future looked bright! Until I was summoned to the CO's office, occupied by a strapping West Pointer of the Jewish faith. With the First Sergeant, a Bataan Death March survivor present, he made it crystal clear that my military basketball "career" was over, forthwith. I was going to soldier, and "Not become a basketball bum." ("OY VEY," I said to myself, recalling a learned Yiddish expression!)

This very unhappy camper saluted and walked out, fighting the temptation to say something stupid. Two weeks later the order came down from Army Headquarters: all cooks, chefs, clerical personnel, special service personnel (i.e., basketball players), "Johnny, get your gun, get your gun, cause your going over." The Chinese had crossed the Yalu and were now in South Korea.

It was stunning news; I thus fully appreciated the huge Roll of Irish Luck, caused by the CO's decision; especially when I later learned that a depressing number of my brother soldiers, so ordered, gave the ultimate sacrifice.

The 529th Signal Company, of which I became a member, was transferred to then Camp Carson, Colorado, just outside picturesque Colorado Springs, renowned for the overhanging and impressive Pikes Peak. (One summer's day, I went to the top, the temperature in Colorado Springs was eighty-two degrees, twenty-eight at the summit).

I wasn't interested in immediately going to Colorado, so I managed to delay the inevitable and enrolled in the Army's Information and Education training program. The fact that it's New Rochelle, New York location was a mere twenty minutes from my Bronx home was not, of course, a consideration. Sure!

By the time I graduated from the program, I had less than a year to go before I responded to the famed suggestion, "Go West, Young Man."

I became an amateur entrepreneur during my stay in Colorado. I found that one could purchase, at wholesale, previously polished U.S. Army insignia buttons at a Manhattan outlet. Wearing them almost ensured a weekend pass at inspection time. I brought a supply back to the Camp and went visiting the black barracks, which were still segregated. I literally couldn't keep them in supply. I had thus discovered my entrepreneurial bent. Where I got that, is anybody's guess. I was discharged on November 22, 1952, a lot thinner and wiser than when I entered.

In the words of the old Irish ditty, "I'm goin' on the Police Farce, it's the only ting ta do!" I was off to the experience of a lifetime: a New York City cop. And would ye believe the shield number they gave him was 911? It was June 1, 1953.

That shield number was first issued in 1895, when New York's finest all wore Charlie Chaplin type helmets. But the catastrophe on 9/11 changed all that. As far as I am concerned, that shield is now a unique icon, honoring all of my fallen brothers.

Many of my childhood friends were in the same Police Academy class, so the rigors of training were facilitated via our irrepressible Bronx humor, epitomized by one of my closest friends, Al LaPerch, who went on to become a department legend. Our class was the first to switch from the olive drab rookie uniform to the current NYPD blue color.

In order to bring that change to the attention of the general public, via the newspaper media, the Police Commissioner George Monaghan contacted the editorial offices of the major newspapers, one of which was the *NY Daily Mirror* (since defunct). My wife to be, Marjorie Rivers, just happened to be the Secretary to Hinson Stiles, the paper's editor. Long story short, I wound up being the department model for an old and new picture-taking session, with the commissioner looking on. When I saw the photo in the next day's edition, I pulled a Jackie Gleason, shouting to all (who weren't really listening), "I'm famous!"

Paraphrasing Victor Hugo's quote on fame, a wise rapper, might say, "Fame? That's just quick, chump change, man!"

The police academy training course was outstanding, given the resources of that day. Instructors made it crystal clear, however, that the career we were embarking upon would make certain the old adage:

"A POLICEMAN'S LOT IS AN UNHAPPY ONE."

I found that to be true. But, you know, I wouldn't trade a minute for the satisfaction of having been an NYPD cop and having been a part of its iconic, "Band of (Blue) Brothers"; it's fair to say that most any other cop, the world over, thinks the same way about their career.

Upon graduation, I was assigned to the 41st Precinct, the very same that I had spent my formative years. When I entered the station house, I bumped in Patrolman Al Davis, who used to walk me across the street as a kid at St. Martin's Grammar School. He was the classic neighborhood cop, cordial, very able, and blessed with a wry sense of humor.

When I rode with him in the radio car a few times, he imparted bits of wisdom about the way to handle the inevitable family fight calls I would experience. "Never take sides," he cautioned and, "never lose sight of the husband's hands."

He also said, "You're going to be exposed to a dark side of Irish drinking, unlike anything you've seen in your home," meaning that when many suffering Irish women had enough of their husband's drinking and/or carrying on, they dialed the equivalent of the then nonexistent 911 system. Italian women were not so inclined. Therefore, most family fight calls in the precinct were blarney-related, if you will.

I had to bite my lip every time the burly Irish Sergeant began to turn us out for patrol duty. His priceless brogue boomed, "Aall 'rite men, lyne up, tooo tic!" (Translation: All right, men line up, two thick.)

The same Sergeant pulled up to me in his radio car one day when I was on street patrol, standing in front of a cigar store. He said, "Caulfield, go in dere and get yourself a couple of good cigars, caaz yur goin' to need em." Huh?

I was introduced then to the terrible stench of a dead, swollen body, rotting for two weeks in an apartment during an August heat wave. I was left alone in the apartment with my cigar fix, successfully fought nausea for two hours, until the Medical Examiner arrived. I never fully got the odor out of that uniform, eventually discarding it in frustration.

My first beat was located on Arthur Avenue, famed for authentic Sicilian food. The Half Moon restaurant there had at that time, in my opinion, the best pizza in New York City. The bookmakers were delighted with my arrival, because many of their customers instantly began playing my 911 shield number.

I had no sooner graduated from the Police Academy, when my passion to become a detective began. I was elated when after nine months of foot patrol, I was regularly assigned to a patrol car, covering the west side of the precinct. I relished the thought of the action inherent in that type of work, and knew my chances of getting in the bureau would be increased.

Listening to the action going on was fascinating, especially on a Saturday night in the 41st Precinct, better known as "Fort Apache." Those radio car guys really earned their pay.

One night we got a call for a male disturbance in a bar. When we arrived with four other sector cars, we found a little more than a mere disturbance. An out-of-his-mind drunken patron was crouched on the bar floor with two broken whiskey bottles in his hands, cursing, screaming, and challenging anyone of us who wished to take him on. I immediately deferred to the old timers, who certainly had seen a variation of that insanity.

That was, of course, before today's pepper spray products. One veteran instantly came up with a simple, non-intrusive solution. He uncapped a bottle of Pepsi Cola, poured a little out and shook thoroughly, capped it with his thumb, preventing the heavy stream from exiting the bottle, until he was within four feet of the deranged guy. Then he let it fly. It worked, momentarily distracting him enough for the rest of us to jump him and get the broken bottles out of his hand. Still fighting, I hit him on his shins (as taught in the police academy) with my PD issue baton, which instantly broke into splinters. The next day I bought a Cocobolo replacement, the hardest wood baton one could buy. I think they would call the whole incident living and learning the hard way.

Nothing was quite like the adrenalin rush I experienced when, on my very first day in a radio car, my partner, Hilty Spokony, and I heard the pulse rattling call: "In the four-six precinct, assist patrolman, shots fired, Fordham Road and Jerome Avenue." For the first time, I drew my revolver from its holster.

With siren blaring, we arrived first on the scene. But it was already over. The patrolman, Vincent Langan, was standing, visibly shaken, over the body of a mob contract killer, later identified as Edward "Snakes" Ryan. Incredibly, Vincent, in the furious gun battle that had ensued, missed with his first six revolver shots and took cover behind a vehicle in order to reload, with Snakes still shooting at him with his multi-round automatic.

Clearly out gunned, he had time to put only one round into the chamber. He fired and, with a shot between Snakes' eyes (sorry!), killed him instantly. By the time we arrived, all Vincent wanted was a triple shot of booze, which I ran and got from the corner saloon.

We quickly learned that Snakes was reported to have been seen fleeing from a nearby tenement apartment house, where pistol shots were heard.

Langan, on traffic duty nearby, quickly responded; he encountered Snakes running through St. James Park with a pistol in his hand.

The still-panicked residents of the apartment house told us there was a body just outside the elevator on the sixth floor. The deceased was subsequently identified as a union leader, for whom mafia elements had farmed out that particular hit to the now infamous Snakes. Lots of press inquiry and investigations followed.

Vincent was appropriately decorated and publicly awarded a detective Gold Shield by the Police Commissioner, who also gave him an instant promotion from the normal detective 3rd grade position to a coveted detective, 2nd grade rank. The irony was that he was working as a newly assigned Bronx traffic cop, close by the mentioned apartment house, when the incident occurred. He had asked for and just received a transfer to traffic duty because he wanted to get away from the unnerving violence he was witnessing as a cop in Harlem's 28th Precinct!

Back to radio car work: in September 1955, my partner and I were on the alert for a guy who thought holding up ten drug stores in our precinct was a good idea. We had a good description, when my clever Irish partner, Timothy Moriarty (another of the few Irish cops on the "Farce") and I, spotted him on a street corner. We threw him in the car and before we had gone three blocks, he confessed and I was off to the detective bureau; it was October 1, 1955.

My mother's cousin, Lt. Ed Gannon, the detective squad commander in my precinct, in a very much appreciated gesture, made it known to the chief of detectives that I not only had some college (not too many did), and a Spanish language qualification. I had taken Spanish in high school, and my teacher, Mr. Gonzalez, was also a basketball buff. So I guess, it can be retrospectively said: "*Ay Caramba! La lingua Espanol es importante!*"

When I was told that I was to be resultantly assigned to the very elite detective unit, the Bureau of Special Services and Investigations (BOSSI), I said, "What the hell is that?" That, for me, turned out to be the profound experience of my police career, for the elite unit had two main missions: (a) protecting heads of state and the President (along with the Secret Service), during their visits to the City, and (b) conduct investigations in to the activities of potentially dangerous groups operating within the City. That activity was often in concert with the FBI. I was about to enter a world I hardly knew existed.

My detective career began at age twenty-six, with smoke coming out of my ears. But the first thing I had to learn was HOW to investigate. The detective school criterion was excellent. I remember one great lesson on the credibility of witnesses. During a lecture, a small Latino worker came in unannounced and unobtrusively replaced a light bulb. As soon as he left the instructor told us fledgling "super" investigators to write down a detailed description of him. He read them to the class, who uproariously reacted to the descriptions, which were unbelievably varied. Case made and closed!

My first investigative assignment was to work with the NYC Department of Investigations. This was the time of the McCarthy era and a commissioner got the idea that there were a number of existing or former Communist teachers in the Department of Education. He was right; and unfortunately for them the Communist Party was put on the ballot from the time of the 1936 election.

All that was necessary was to prove a teacher was a Communist sympathizer was to search the NYC election records, and if he/she denied it under oath, they were gone. The only thing I learned from that experience was that public records were an important investigatory tool.

I learned the tedious process of verifying health, criminal, credit, and motor vehicle records, which could take a week or more per individual. It is almost laughable today, when such work can now accomplished within three to five mouse clicks.

Shortly after taking up my BOSSI duties, I was informed that, because of my Spanish language qualification, I was to work on a new case with the FBI involving an unregistered Cuban agent, named Arnaldo Barron, who reported to none other than a guy named, Fidel Castro; who was then conducting his revolution in the remote mountains, of western Cuba.

Barron was charged with a federal violation of the Foreign Agents Registration Act, and was readily convicted. I got to testify as a government witness at his trial in Washington, D.C., and was starting to put my chest out; not very smart.

Sometime thereafter, I was tracking one Jesus Yanez Pelletier, a key Castro gunrunner, before Fidel took power on January 1, 1959. We were close to nailing him, but history intervened. I met him as he was boarding a plane to celebrate in Havana on that date. He was, excuse the pun, flying pretty high.

The next time I saw him was when Castro came to the UN in September 1959. He had emerged as Fidel's Chief of Security. With his intelligence, outstanding military background, and bearing, it looked like Fidel made a good choice, except for the inevitable paranoia and jealousies surrounding all despotic regimes.

Long story short, Raul Castro, brother of Fidel, saw to it that Jesus was given a not-so-pleasant, fifteen-year "vacation" in Cuba's notorious Isle of Pines prison. Now, that's hard time!

Apparently, the underlying motivation for his imprisonment was for having an affair with a Castro mistress, Marita Lorenz, after he was ordered to arrange for the abortion of Castro's illegitimate child in Manhattan. Lorenz, daughter of a German sea captain, was also enmeshed as a principal in a failed, bizarre Castro assassination plot, funded by the CIA; allegedly with the complicity of the Italian mob and knowledge of Robert Kennedy, then the U.S. Attorney General. Stuff like that has conspiracy theorists smiling when they go to bed at night. (Note: Castro has always been silent on the subject of abortion, perhaps because of the family scandal that he was born the illegitimate child of a woman then a servant in the Castro household?)

To Jesus' credit, when he finally emerged from the nightmare, he became a most effective enemy of Castro and Raul. In the process, he gave highly damaging insights into the political treachery of the regime, along with personal habit revelations/intrigues, etc., regarding the brothers, about which one could only be disgusted. Jesus died recently, with a clear conscience, I am sure.

In 1957 I got a call from sharp, first-grade detective, John Weber of the 34th detective squad. He said he had a weird one. In his squad room, a Latino in custody was singing for his freedom by giving up two Jewish kids from Brooklyn, engaged in an illegal gunrunning scam. In giving up the sellers, he identified a New Jersey gun store owner, from whom the scam artists purportedly bought the guns. Off we went to see the owner. Lo and behold, it was Dave Lang. I graduated from Rice High School with him!

We, thus, quickly got the accurate story about the Brooklyn scammers, who were picking up extra change by selling trophy Thompson Sub Machine guns that had been deactivated (to qualify for trophy status) as the real McCoy.

The difference between the trophy price and the McCoy price made it worth the Brooklyn entrepreneurs' while. However, if the metal piece causing the deactivation was not removed from the barrel, the gun would blow up in the shooter's face. Their first selling target was an alleged IRA member living in the Bronx.

His name was John Faughey, then residing at 2134 Plimpton Avenue in the Bronx. As we were heading back to the Bronx, I told my partner, Ray Clark, that I thought my Uncle Mike lived in that very same building and I wasn't going to give my name during the interview; sure enough, the vestibule directory indicated Mike Caulfield was a tenant in apartment number thirty-three. Faughey's name was indicated at apartment number thirty-one. WHOOPS!

It took about two minutes after he opened his door for him to begin his crying confession. It turned out that he was a member of a small, independent anti-Brit group, known as the Northern Republican Society, perhaps loosely connected to the IRA cause. That night my mother told me that Faughey, my uncle, and father arrived in the United States from Ireland on the same day, together.

Thus, with good reason, I never brought the subject up with my father, for it was more than possible that my Uncle Mike had knowledge of the activities, who subsequently beat the rap and the Brooklyn kids paid a fine. Improperly handled, I could have started an O'Hatfield/O'McCoy (pun intended!) feud! In any event, while it was not the heaviest case in the history of the NYPD, I certainly won't be forgetting it anytime soon.

That incident became part of my Watergate testimony in May of 1973. I listed the police commendations I had received, including the above, without further explanation. That night, the then President of the New York City Council, Paul O'Dwyer, a onetime lawyer for the mafia-corrupt International Longshoreman's Union, raged in the press that I was a "traitor to the Irish cause!" I wondered if his rage was because I didn't give a wave to illegal guns being sent to Ireland!

He didn't have a clue about the above facts behind that commendation. Not that I intended it to be so, of course, but our arrest actually precluded Irish fighters from being killed or maimed by the Faughey-purchased, ready-to-malfunction Thompson (trophy) guns. So there, Paul!

Note: Coincidentally, one of the leading all-time, Irish rebel songs is entitled, "The Thompson Gun." The fact that the famous weapon was invented by an Englishman, John Thompson, didn't bother the Irish authors.

While there is no greater insult to an Irishman than to have that false charge leveled publicly, I found myself laughing at the stupidity of the comment, resisting the temptation to go down to City Hall and, if not give him a punch in the mouth, at least call the press and remind them about his brother, Bill, who became a NYPD cop, Police Commissioner, and eventually Mayor.

When publicly alleged to have been tied to mafia corruption in 1950, he summarily resigned the mayoralty post and found the perfect job and place to hide from further inquiry: after being nominated by President Truman, Bill Faughey became the U.S. Ambassador to Mexico. Both brothers are now dead, so it's best to leave well enough alone.

Later in my detective career, I asked for and received a transfer to the Bronx Homicide Squad after I felt I was unfairly passed over for a preferred BOSSI assignment with the New York mayor's protective detail. To say the least, grunt homicide work was a sea change from the rarified BOSSI VIP security work.

I was back to smoking cigars again, when I learned that any suspicious death meant a working homicide detective had to be pro forma-present at the deceased's autopsy. Such duty does not increase one's appetite! The medical examiner's nurse, present at all such autopsy's, was privately and jokingly nicknamed "Slug" to those of us who certainly didn't admire her position, but respected her forbearance under daily testing circumstances.

In any event, I caught my first case in the "Fort Apache" precinct on August 22, 1966, a steamy hot day. The deceased, a Latino bodega owner was apparently slain by a black male youth seen fleeing from the scene. Fortuitously, the crime scene was pristine because the deceased's son, upon finding the body, ran to tell relatives and had locked the entrance door as he left.

The first thing I noticed was an open orange juice container next to the cash register, which led me to an early guess that the killer was the purchaser prior to stabbing the owner to death in an ensuing scuffle. Looking close at the container, but not touching it, I saw a barley distinct fingerprint, which was preserved from the ninety-five degree heat outside when the bodega door was locked.

We quickly got a lab technician to the scene, who told us he was able to safely remove one finger print for possible future analysis. At that time, one fingerprint could not get you an I.D., unless you knew the name of the suspect and could compare it to a recorded set of prints.

We began the investigation in a normal fashion, tracing the killer's flight from the scene and canvassing neighbors in that area, which revealed that he, had run to a nearby El Station.

With nothing else to go on, the hard work of trying to come up with street information began. Since the crime scene was in a Puerto Rican neighborhood and the black killer fled to a subway train, the chances were that he did not live near the crime scene.

We began by identifying and speaking to known drug dealers and junkies, always vulnerable to a coercive deal if the price was right, e.g., "Give up the guy we are looking for and then we can talk about your problem."

After a couple of false drug-dealer leads, we were nowhere a month after the killing. I wasn't happy. And then Irish Luck began to roll. Out of the blue, we got a call that there was a black youth in the Brooklyn House of Detention on a burglary charge who wanted to sing about the guy who killed the Puerto Rican. Out we went to interview him. He said that one of his friends told him that Jimmy (few knew last names in Fort Apache!), a purported black junkie living in the precinct, did it. Hmmm.

We go back and do find a Jimmy who fit the description given, but had a good alibi, which we tended to believe. Around that time, I remembered a wise lesson from detective school—always investigate your informants. So, I said to myself, it might not be a bad idea for me to call my buddy, Jimmy Bannon, who worked with me earlier in my patrol car career and was now in the NYPD's fingerprint section.

I asked him since we had this partial print on the orange juice container, would he compare it to the prints of our jailhouse informer and let me know. Thirty minutes later, Jim called and said, "You got him, Jack, it's a perfect match." Yahoo!

Back we went to see our informer, with the orange juice container in my briefcase. He said, "How you guys do?"

I said, as I simultaneously put the container on the desk in front of him, "We did great, but YOU, man, are going away for fifteen mother------ years!" (This was not time for the Kings English!) He rolled his head and eyes backwards, to a point that I only saw the whites of his eyes.

All told, I caught eleven homicide cases during my tenure in the squad. I solved all except the last because they were relative pieces of cake—family fights, drug deals gone sour, known thieves, etc. However, that last case personified "the policeman's lot" syndrome for me.

It began as an atypical, drug-related homicide. The deceased was a lowly, black female drug dealer, who, when arrested, made the huge mistake of threatening, via conversation with friends, to give up her supplier, an Italian tied to the mob, which suggested that there might be bigger fish involved in that case.

That trail led to a guy named Marty Yamin, a clever Baltimore thief tied to the mob drug running and married to a member of the Dominican Republic's Mission to the United Nations. We installed a legal wiretap on Yamin's phone in Manhattan. Initially there were three detectives, including myself, charged with the daily monitoring process.

Then, after the case began to take on a mob/diplomatic flavor, we got word that a Bronx police superior had caused another detective to be assigned to the case. That detective, then involved in narcotics work, had previously worked for AT&T, before joining the department. His assignment to the case, while unusual, was somewhat accepted because of his prior telephone experience.

But a corrupt atom bomb went off on a Saturday morning when I was monitoring, in real time, a Yamin conversation initiated by an Italian mafia member living in the Bronx, who we had just identified as a Yamin drug associate. That gave rise to the possibility he was the Italian drug dealer we were looking for. The new member of our team was also aware of the information.

Suddenly, we heard a loud bang, an apparent electrical sound, on the line that was unrelated to their conversation, but more importantly, unrelated to our wiretap! Yamin instantly and correctly recognized the sound for what it was; he screamed, "Son of a bitch! They're tapping your phones!"

I was utterly stunned, too, at the sound. I played the tape over and over after their conversation ended, and came to the same conclusions as Yamin: somebody, at that moment, was screwing around with the mob guy's telephone in the Bronx! And then the terrible dark thought hit me: could it possibly be that our AT&T detective was illegally wiretapping the mob guy's phone . . . for a shakedown purpose . . . at the behest of his police superior!?"

I shuddered at my thoughts, but quickly brought my two able homicide partners to the wiretap location for their review of the tape. They went pale too, as they realized that my assumption not only had significant merit, but was likely right on the money (pun regretfully intended).

It fell to me to advise my homicide commander of our consensus. I knew I was putting him in an awful spot. A potentially career-ending, nasty public scandal was laid on our commander's door step. His shock was also evident when the importance of what I was telling him registered in its entirety. With apparent reluctance he said, "Jack, you just can't make that unequivocal assumption based upon what you are telling me."

I knew then I was really under the gun; however, bracing myself, I replied, "Lieutenant, I'm sorry, but I just did . . . and that's my unequivocal position."

At that moment, I felt that my detective career might well be over. Seriously challenging a police official's integrity, with what might be considered a circumstantial assertion, was, at that time, a certain "kiss of death" for anyone having the temerity to do so. And I just did. Whew!

As I sat around in March of that year (1968), worrying when the proverbial shoe might fall, I received a stunning piece of good news. It emanated from my observation in late 1967, that Richard Nixon was going to run again in 1968 and would, as a private citizen, need a personal security capability when that occurred.

I was assigned to him, as a BOSSI detective, along with the Secret Service, during his 1960 Presidential campaign visits to NYC, and had come to know his able, loyal secretary Rose Woods and Jack Sherwood, who was in charge of Nixon's vice presidential secret service detail at that time.

I made it known to Sherwood that I could probably get a leave of absence, in the event they needed my security services. He advised that, because of advancing age and the demanding physical rigors of a presidential campaign, he was not going to go through that demanding drill again in the upcoming campaign. Gratuitously, he said he would bring my availability to the attention of Rose and Bob Haldeman, then the key Nixon official on the fledgling campaign staff.

On March 23, I found myself being interviewed by Haldeman and Rose at the Nixon campaign headquarters, 57th Street and Park Avenue in Manhattan. I gave them my resume, detailing by BOSSI experience, including an abbreviated list of some one hundred plus presidential, head of state, and foreign VIP security assignments. The interview went well.

Haldeman, apparently impressed, asked if I could arrange for a leave of absence in order to take up Nixon security chief duties for the upcoming campaign. I went to see the able Chief of Detectives, Fred Lussen, who heartily approved the request, stating such an assignment would be an honor for the department. So, the deal was done and happily, I could walk away from that dark cloud overhanging the Bronx Homicide Squad.

But before I get to the chapter on the 1968 campaign, let me take you, in the next chapter, to some other interesting BOSSI experiences involving my VIP security assignments and sometimes associated investigations, into terrorists and/or radical political groups.

Chapter 2: BOSSI

When the United Nations building opened its doors in 1950, it ensured that many heads of state and lesser dignitaries would be frequent visitors to the City of New York. The U.S. State Department created a special security division to respond to that development.

Reacting similarly, the NYPD's detective division established, in 1952, the Bureau of Special Services and Investigations (BOSSI), to work with the State Department's entity and the security services of the VIP visitor. Alternatively, the unit worked in conjunction with the U.S. Secret Service, when the president or vice president, and/or their families visited the city.

An additional charge for the unit was to conduct investigations into radical organizations, when such activities rose to atypical status and posed a threat to good order within the city.

A precursor unit, Special Squad #1, existed during the thirties and forties. Its members investigated and when necessary penetrated, among others, the German Bund and the Communist Party; both were headquartered within Manhattan, and, at that time, represented potentially serious threats to not only the United States, but the city as well.

On that note, I found it interesting to learn that a co-founder of the Russian Revolution, Leon Trotsky, had, according to a *Bronx Home News* (a newspaper I delivered in my youth) headline of that day, "Bronx Man Leads Russian Revolution." His revolutionary headquarters was located at 1522 Vyse Avenue. That location was no more than a few blocks from my family's Bronx residence; making it a close-to-home, small-world story.

The FBI's arrests of Nazi saboteurs off Long Island and the Soviet atomic spy ring participants, led by the Ethel and Julius Rosenberg of Manhattan, speak to those threats. Special Squad #1 members worked closely with the FBI in those and other related matters. BOSSI detectives Mildred Blauvelt and Stephanie Horvath were cited by congressional committees for their commendable work in that regard as well. My first VIP security assignment, a.k.a. escort, was the UN visit of Jawaharlal Nehru, the Prime Minister of India in 1956. At that time, there was no formal security training for such an assignment by the NYPD. You just showed up and learned by the seat of your pants. I quickly found the best way to accelerate knowledge was to watch the unit's pros, like detective Ray Clark, previously mentioned.

He had experience guarding a number of VIP's, including General Douglas McArthur, when he received a tumultuous ticker-tape welcome after summary dismissal from military service by President Truman. He was also a key part of John F. Kennedy's BOSSI security team in the 1960 election, which I will get into a little later.

Note: Ray's uncle, PJ Clark founded a Manhattan saloon by the same name, which is still a well-known luncheon and drinking hangout for New Yorkers of every persuasion. Its turn-of-the-century urinals give new visitors something to giggle about.

Another pro was Frank Cresci, a socially smooth detective, fluent in French and Italian. BOSSI bosses assigned him to Prince Ranier of Monaco, when he first came to the city. Ranier's full name was: Ranier-Louis-Henri-Maxense-Bertrand de Grimaldi. (Sounds royal to me!)

Over the years on that continuing assignment, Cresci witnessed firsthand Ranier's courtship and eventual marriage to the Irish bricklayer's daughter, Grace Kelly. When he retired, he became a Monaco official at their Consul General's office in Manhattan.

Nehru, who succeeded the assassinated Mahatma Gandhi as India's leader, was, like so many national leaders to follow, happy to use the UN platform to create a positive image at home and abroad. I certainly did not care about that. I remember thinking as my first escort began was, "What the hell do I do now?"

One of the first stops on Nehru's itinerary was at the Waldorf Astoria, where he spoke and mingled with guests at a political luncheon, heavily covered by the media. I recognized that no State Department or BOSSI security person was in appropriate proximity to him. Intuitively, I took a position close enough to him to provide security in the unlikely event of an incident, but not so obvious that my presence would be unduly noticed by the media.

My sergeant boss at the time saw the move; later commenting positively, saying it was timely and made sense. He made his observation known to Frank Robb, the CO of the BOSSI unit. So began my career in VIP security.

During my eleven-year (1955 to 1966) BOSSI tenure, I participated in close to 100 security escorts, most involving lesser-known dignitaries. While many were routine, a few were more than interesting and some downright dangerous. Indicated below, is a short list of some of those assignments, coupled with my observations. They are in no particular order.

The visit of the President of Ireland, Sean T. O'Kelly to New York, on March 19 through 20, 1959, was one I will not forget. He had just come from a visit to the White House, where, on St. Patrick's Day, he presented President Eisenhower with a pro-forma gift of shamrocks; and then addressed the U.S. Congress. He's pictured below with Vice President Nixon looking on in his official capacity as President of the U.S. Senate.

The New York Irish were delirious and gave him a thunderous welcome at his ticker-tape parade on the twentieth. As part of his security entourage at that event, I was in a front-page photo, walking next to his limousine as it moved up the financial canyon to City Hall. The Caulfield "clan" in New York, Ireland, and other points of the Irish Diaspora, was resultantly "proud as punch," as one might imagine.

After a visit to the UN, he returned to his suite at the Waldorf Astoria. The head of his delegation called me aside and said, "Jack, the president will make a very private visit to St. Steven's church this evening. He wants no publicity, so it will be his car with an aide and just two detectives from your office. Okay?"

I said, "Fine with me, Eileen."

Off we went in a silent, two-car motorcade to the nearby church. At its altar, he knelt and said a private prayer. Unexpectedly, however, when he rose, his aide took him by the arm to a door adjacent to the altar, which led to a darkened staircase.

Huh? I looked quizzically at the aide; whose "shush" finger motion reassured me that what was occurring was part of some kind of plan. When we reached the bottom of the stairwell, the aide knocked on a nearby door.

When it opened, the lights went on in a large room, revealing an assembly of over 300 former IRA comrades of the president!

Simultaneously, they all broke into a robust, tearful rendition of the heart throbbing, "Soldiers Song," the Irish National Anthem. At its end, wild cheering and more tears went on and on for minutes. Finally, he waved them to silence and his first booming words were, "Fifty years ago . . . here in Manhattan . . . the Irish rebellion was born!"

Everyone there knew what he meant. I found out later that it was O'Kelly who, in 1909, as a young official in the Dublin-based "Sinn Fein" political organization, initiated and engineered a critical fundraising effort in New York. Without his success, the armed 1917 Easter Rebellion in "Dublin's Fair City" might not have occurred. The Irish have words for it, "Erin Go Bragh," meaning, "Ireland Forever."

Assigned to the Queen of England's ticker-tape parade on October 21, 1957, I was likewise photographed next to the limousine transporting her and husband, Prince Phillip. When that photo appeared in the papers the next day, my father's reaction was not proud as punch; rather, I think, the single word "punch," came to his mind.

Getting up close, but not personal, with the Royals was interesting. I watched as Prince Philip told a sexist joke to male associates in a Waldorf Astoria elevator, indicating to me that he puts his pants on one leg at a time, just like everyone else.

The Queen's sister, Princess Margaret (now deceased) and her then husband, the Lord Earl of Snowdon (formerly Anton Armstrong Jones), came to the city for a private visit just prior to their divorce.

They stayed at an upscale townhouse on Manhattan's East Side. Their itinerary told us they were going to party that evening in the Big Apple, as was their wont. However, the New York arm of the IRA had other ideas; they demonstrated in a loud and boisterous manner, hurling anti-Brit epithets, well within earshot of the apartment. In a royal huff, they jumped into their Rolls Royce, very much like that pictured in the below photo.

Their destination was a British government estate on Long Island, where they would spend a, probably unwanted, quiet weekend. As we neared the security jurisdiction turnover point on the Long Island Expressway, the right rear door of the Rolls flew open, causing its driver to brake quickly and pull onto the shoulder. We raced out of our follow-up vehicle and looked inside.

Neither was hurt, but it was an eye-opening scene. The Princess was disheveled and crying uncontrollably. Snowdon plaintively cried out more than once, "I don't know what happened . . . it JUST flew open!" It appeared to us that they had some sort of shoving match in their vehicle, (not readily visible from our follow-up vehicle) with Snowdon, appearing intoxicated, accidentally kicking the door open.

Anyway, that was his story, and as they say in the Bronx, he was sticking to it. That stance might not have resolved the marital dispute, but it sure got the attention of senior Rolls Royce executives, who jumped on the first jet from London to New York.

They got a department statement from us, as described above. I am sure they turned the vehicle upside down looking for a non-existent flaw in their well-engineered door. In any event, it was nice know that it was not only the Irish who experienced alcohol-related family fights.

When Philippine President Carlos P. Garcia came to New York on June 6, 1959 for a UN visit and ticker-tape parade, I was a BOSSI security team member. Upon his departure, everyone on the security team received a gift of high quality cigars, contained in a handsomely designed box. I told my mother I thought it would be a great idea to give that gift to our local dry cleaner, who was born in the Philippines. She agreed, so I gave it him. His tears of appreciation, after I handed it to him, moved me as well.

In May 1962, Sardar Mohammod Daoud, Prime Minister of Afghanistan, arrived in the city for a UN visit. He was reputed to be a brutal leader who took total power from a relative in a bloodless coup. His government initially sided with the West, but later aligned itself with the Soviets, in the seventies. In 1978, he was assassinated in a counter coup.

In the ninety's, Taliban resistance forces, led by al-Qaeda and the then-emerging Osama Bin Laden, using sophisticated heat-seeking missiles supplied by the U.S. Pentagon, blew Russian military helicopters out of the Afghan sky and then out of the country with tails between their Cossack boots. Those were the good old days!

Getting back to his visit, he decided he wanted to go shopping at Macy's department store on 34th Street in Manhattan. One of his UN aides, appearing near apoplectic in his presence, was in charge of steering his boss around Macy's aisles. He may have sealed his diplomatic fate by obsequiously over doing it, taking an embarrassing header, when he tripped over a box. Daoud gave him a look that, realistically, could kill.

President Sukarno of Indonesia came to New York for a ticker-tape parade on May 22, 1956, and stayed at the Waldorf Astoria. That was a tense time for the Eisenhower administration in that Sukarno was receiving military aid from both the United States and the USSR, and the future of Sukarno's loyalties were in doubt.

Apparently, the CIA knew he had a sexual character flaw, which wasn't really a secret. I was there when some CIA people were seen bringing a few fast-looking (spells: hooker) females to his presidential suite during his two-day stay there.

Further, I recently read an apparently reliable press account of a government archived report. It indicated that the CIA successfully recruited a sophisticated American woman and induced her into creating an ongoing sexual liaison with Sukarno from which the CIA purportedly gained valuable information.

Some have speculated she fell in love with Sukarno and perhaps became the modern day equivalent of the famous WWI sexual spy, Mata Hari, a double agent for the Germans working against her handlers, the French, who executed her in 1917.

Political intrigues, as one might imagine, were also rampant at the UN amongst national Intelligence entities working that fertile turf. The UN's security entity usually gave a Christmas party attended by members of those entities based in New York. Some of us working in BOSSI were invited as well.

What impressed me most was the high quality of the operatives working out of the Soviet Mission to the UN in Manhattan. These were not grunt types, running around with Kalashnikov weapons at the ready. Their suave social demeanor and mastery of the English language, without a discernable accent, was such that one would almost think he was talking with a California native. I doubt, however, they could have pulled off "Da Bronx" accent.

When Nikita Khrushchev, the Soviet leader, came to town for a UN visit in September 1960, the U.S. State Department security team decided to host a late-night drinking party at a Manhattan bistro for their competitor Soviet team, which included the above mentioned operatives.

The idea was to get the Soviet attendees drunk enough so that the "loose lips, sinks ships" WWII caveat became fully operational . . . for our side. We probably lost that one, given the well-known penchant (well exhibited that night) of Russians to down huge quantities of vodka and keep rolling along with nary a misspoken word.

When we returned to Khrushchev's presidential suite at the Waldorf Towers at about 3:00 a.m., the uniformed cop stationed directly outside the suite (believe it or not, the only security person on that floor at that hour) was sitting, sound asleep, with feet up on a second chair for maximum comfort.

Anyone could have gone through the unlocked door and said, "Hi Nikita!" One State Department security agent started yelling as if he wanted the cop's head, or at least to cause him an instant transfer to the Bronx's 50th precinct, then a form of semi-retirement.

Fortunately for the cop, the head of that State security team was Leo Crampsey, a former football All-American at St. Bonaventure and an NFL player. While he calmed the red-faced agent, I talked like a brother to the cop, who must have rubbed his rabbit's foot more than a few times, in that we let that "sleeping rabbit" lie.

Leo, now deceased, was my man. If there ever was a hero in the VIP security business, it was Crampsey. He can be aptly described as fearless and I am proud to say he became a close friend. I was also deeply indebted to him for all of the invaluable mentoring he gave when I was a clueless young detective on the BOSSI team.

On that same visit, Khrushchev, after his famous table-pounding scene in the UN General Assembly, was sounding off to the world's media from the balcony on the Soviet Mission's Park Avenue location. Suddenly, a KGB security agent whipped out a camera and started taking photos of us "Gringo" (how do you say that in Russian?) security agents.

I was standing next to Leo, trying to think of something smart to say. He "one-upped" everyone by quickly grabbing a camera from a U.S. Army Counter Intelligence Corps agent present at the surreal scene. He shouted, with "Patton-esque" authority, "Hey, son of a bitch, this one's for you!" and proceeded to photograph him and every other KGB agent in the area.

Even they got a good laugh at Leo's action . . . it was that type of "in your face" (pun intended) reaction they fully understood.

At the time of the Tet Offensive in January 1968, Leo was a State Department security official at the U.S. Embassy in Saigon. In a now-famous video clip, Leo is seen in street clothes outside the embassy, directing embassy-assigned Marines, while also firing an automatic weapon directly into an Embassy window. The Viet Cong, at that moment, had partial internal control of the embassy. He properly received the State Department's highest award for his heroism.

Leo also had an infectious sense of humor, coupled with a talent to tell a good story. He had me bending over with this one. He said he was on duty one night, standing outside the Organization of American States building in Washington, D.C., when an apparently intoxicated Lyndon Johnson, then a senator, came out looking for his vehicle.

Johnson did not know Leo (who stood six feet and three inches tall, and weighed 220 pounds) at that time, but said in an authoritative voice, "Hey you, you look big and stupid enough; go get my (blankety-blank) car!"

Leo responded with an instant, "Yes Sir!" and then proceeded to the parking lot, got in HIS own car, and went home. There was only one Leo Crampsey.

Leo and I traveled in a 1964 motorcade when Johnson, then president, exited the UN and was on his way back to (where else?) the Waldorf Astoria, accompanied by a foreign VIP. Cops and barricades lined the return route to control the cheering crowd. As we neared the hotel, the crowd's decibel level rose; a uniformed cop began to panic as the motorcade approached. I could not believe my eyes as I saw him draw his pistol (whoops!), looking intently for non-existent assassins on the neighboring rooftops. Our eyes were not on phantom assassins, but on the panicked cop. Oh well, we are all far from perfect.

Upon retirement, Leo became chief of security for the DuPont Corporation, in Wilmington, Delaware. They were lucky to get him.

I remember how BOSSI first learned that Khrushchev was coming to the UN. An official at the aforementioned Soviet UN Mission called and asked Frank Robb, our boss at the time, to come up to their mission; he had an important message for him. I drove Robb up there and sat in a waiting room while he went into another room to speak with the official.

On the way, back he gave me the big news: Khruschev was coming to New York. Their politically adept mission people, wanting to CYA, knew the NYPD were the guys to ensure that all would go smoothly, notwithstanding the antics of their controversial leader when he was out and about the city and elsewhere.

Upon our return, Robb had an urgent call from FBI agent Gus Micek, the FBI's able liaison with our office. Sheepishly, Micek advised him that FBI surveillance cameras, located outside the mission, had caught Robb and me entering and leaving the mission.

Robb laughed at the thought of "being caught" on tape by the bureau; he gratuitously gave Micek the stunning Khrushchev news. For me, it was my first insight into the major league world of governmental espionage, engaged in by almost any nation worth its salt.

The Soviets, no saints in that league, pulled off a pretty good one way back in 1952 at our embassy in Moscow by planting what was then a highly sophisticated microphone inside a large wooden replica of the Great Seal of the United States, containing the American eagle, our national symbol.

It was a gift (ha!) to the then U.S. Ambassador to the USSR, and hung in his office and other sensitive locations in the embassy over the years. Remotely controlled by an on/off switch device (unheard of in those days), it was, allegedly, undetectable in the "off" mode.

The FBI materially "one-upped" that impressive caper in the mid-sixties, when their wiretap expert, agent Jack Ragan, created a uniquely discreet telephone system, then had it routed through the Soviet Mission's telephone switchboard; meaning that when it became operational, all worldwide calls in and out of that hive of intrigue were instantly known to the FBI. In my opinion, that was one great piece of work . . . for our side.

Ragan, when retired, went into the corporate security world, providing telephone security services for his clients, one of which was the Nixon, Mudge, Rose, Mitchell, and Alexander law firm in New York (more about his role in the Nixon 1968 presidential campaign later).

One of the more controversial world figures of the 1960s was Marshal Tito of Yugoslavia. His government, sometimes aligned (sometimes not) with the Soviet Union, was nevertheless known to be consistently repressive and brutally harsh on any internal dissidents, especially those clergy of the catholic faith.

When he came to the city for the historical UN General Assembly session of 1960, BOSSI, State security, and UN security were rightly concerned about the potentially dangerous anti-Tito elements operating in New York and elsewhere in the United States. It was a one-time opportunity for those suffering people to demonstrate and publicly vent their rage directly at Tito and his government. The word assassination came to our minds, as well.

Within that context, someone in the NYPD or State Department (I didn't want to know) got the idea that BOSSI's exclusive photographic file on dissident anti-Tito demonstrators in NY should also be made available to the UN Security entity. On the surface, that appeared to be a logical tact, for Tito was certainly security-vulnerable, not only in the city but also when on UN international property, as well. UN security officials made copies of the photos and furnished them to their personnel.

Long story short, via various slips of tongue, we found, to our utter dismay, that a Russian born UN security officer, also known as a "womanizing playboy" by BOSSI detectives, had sold the photographs to Tito's entourage!

Later, dismay compounded to outright disgust when we learned through the FBI that some of the families of those photographed dissidents were tortured and or slain back in Yugoslavia. I am trying to write something morally profound here, but I think the above facts speak, damningly, for themselves.

As far as I know, UN officials did nothing about that travesty. Their despicable creature remained employed there until his retirement. It would be nice; however, if this belated disclosure made a public case for the adage, "The pen is mightier than the sword (of treachery)." Whether it does or does not, I, for one, in this matter, will NEVER leave well enough alone.

To get off that downer, permit me to state that there were occasional moments of high humor involved in BOSSI escort duty. A classic involved Bob Bystricky, a Brooklyn-born, street-smart detective blessed with a great sense of humor. He found his way into the squad because he was fluent in the Czechoslovakian language, emanating from his immigrant Czech parents. If a detective spoke a foreign language, he/she had a leg up on assignment to the elite BOSSI unit.

The antithesis of the aforementioned, Frank Cresci was rough around the social edges but had a passionate desire to join the escort duty part of the squad. A couple of the bosses, seeing the edges, kept putting off his continued requests for such duty, until one day in May 1961 they came up a man short for a Saudi King escort assignment.

Bob was clearly hyper when he joined me and two other detectives on his first assignment. The monarch was staying in the presidential suite at the exclusive Waldorf Towers, part of the famous hotel. The U.S. State Department's chief of protocol led the U.S. entourage. The atmosphere there had a snobbish, diplomatic aura, a world away from Bob's Brooklyn roots; let us include my Bronx roots, too!

As the VIP exited his suite, heading to a prissy social function, Bob went into action before I could stop him. All in the party were properly waiting at the elevator for the subject to enter first. Bob, oblivious to protocol, and quickstepping directly in front of the monarch, gave him a hand wave and a loud, "RIGHT THIS WAY, KING!" He then proceeded to trip and give a great demonstration of a head first slide into second base . . . with the "base" being the inside of the elevator.

I instantly looked at the chief of protocol. His blue blood was rapidly draining from his face; while simultaneously giving the strong impression he was about to barf or worse. Bob never got close to royalty again. Actually, though, he enjoyed retelling this story in his uproarious, quick-witted way more that I did.

Soviet Cosmonaut, Yuri Gagarin, the first human rocketed into space on April 12, 1961, came to the city later that year as part of a public relations tour with Soviet ambassador to the United States, Anatoily Dobrinin, holding his hand. At a couple of private parties he attended, there were numerous American communist sympathizers expressing euphoric delight at his presence; a few were leading American entertainers. There was no question as to where their loyalties lay regarding the critical race for space supremacy; and frankly, I was personally annoyed at their overt displays of affection for Gagarin.

The ambassador effectively put Gagarin in front of New York's media, designed to show the United States and the world how advanced Soviet rocketry was over ours. On the surface, that appeared to be the case, subsequently causing the United States to scramble just to keep up. Americans were rightfully concerned.

I was too . . . until Gagarin and the ambassador reached the entrance door at Idlewild airport as they were departing the city. I was immediately adjacent to both of them at that moment.

As Gagarin reached the door, he stepped on its treadle, just like any six-year-old would in the United States who knew that the door would then open. The difference between a six-year-old and Gagarin was that he had never seen anything like that before!

He instantly became animated and hyper, rattling off exclamatory words to the ambassador, while again and again stepping on the treadle; marveling at how the door continued to open, at the mere push of his foot.

At some point, the ambassador (certainly a long-time airport treadle pusher) was embarrassed enough to end the "demonstration." He gave Yuri a nudge and slight smile, which told him it, was time to go through the door. From then on, I just smiled at those who went through the roof, telling us how we were going to surely lose the technical arms race to the Soviets; even a six-year-old would have known better.

Also on the subject of security at Idlewild airport, I was assigned there to JFK (shortly after he was elected president in 1961), along with the Secret Service. He gave an impromptu talk to union workers in an Idlewild parking lot.

His decision to stop caught both BOSSI and the SS off guard. Following short remarks, he waded into the group to shake hands. There was no security person in his vicinity. Without thinking, I went and took a position close enough to him to be a security presence, in the event of an incident.

There was one, but it did not have to do with JFK; it had to do with me. Secret Service superiors out of Washington, D.C., seeing my move, made a complaint minutes later to the nearby NYPD brass. I was not privy to the conversation, but from where I was standing, I could see that it was somewhat heated.

I later learned their position was that inasmuch as they had primary responsibility for security of the president, and the Secret Service should always clear any presidential security moves undertaken by NYPD members in advance. Therefore, in their view, my conduct was out of order and subject to discipline. Hmm.

The good news for me was that the NYPD brass was not going to have any part of that argument. Their response essentially was, "Look, Caulfield was there, where were your guys?" Touché.

I first met Kennedy when he was still a senator. I was on a BOSSI assignment at the Waldorf Astoria, just weeks before Castro's January 1, 1959 successful over throw of the Batista government. He and his younger brother, Ted, were attending a charity fundraising event there, whose organizers were New York elite. The beneficiaries of the event were to be underprivileged children in Cuba.

The newspaper announcement of that upcoming event got the attention of the FBI and BOSSI. Anti-Batista demonstration activity in the city was peaking at that time, along with reports of an imminent Castro military success. The bosses thus thought it would be prudent to have two detectives who knew leaders and members of the NYC anti-Batista groups assigned to the event as a security contingency. I was one of them.

Kennedy, observing our presence, and correctly figuring we were law enforcement, came and engaged us in conversation. As soon as he learned why we were there, his mind went into overdrive, peppering us with insightful questions about our office's knowledge of the anti-Batista movement in the city. I do not know if we impressed him, but the sharpness of his mind certainly impressed us.

As the conversation ended, we were amused to see his brother dancing with a great looking Cuban entertainer to the tune of "Guadalajara." As I write this, forty-nine years later, news media are playing an audio rendition of the senator singing the same song to Mexican adherents of his immigration bill. As to his singing talent, one might smilingly say, "Senator, you are no John McCormack" (the great Irish tenor).

Someone recently brought to my attention the Kennedy family ancestry, located on the Internet. As I scrolled through the names, I found that a John T. Caulfield (clerk) was married in 1882 to Margaret Kennedy, age twenty-seven, of Boston. She was the daughter of Patrick Kennedy, the great-grandfather of JFK, who came to the United States because of the Irish potato famine in 1848. All that told me was that at least one Caulfield made it to those rarified "Lace Curtain Irish" circles.

I was on the JFK security detail on his last trip to New York, just prior to his assassination. It was a private visit. Staying at the exclusive Carlyle hotel, he decided to walk to his sister's apartment a block away. He was unaccompanied by anyone, other than BOSSI and SS agents stationed along the route. I was in the middle of the block.

As was his style, he wore no overcoat on that chilly, November evening. Thus, I was able to get a good, close-up view of the president as he came towards me, alone, apparently in deep thought. His stunning good looks made a lasting impression, which I took away from that fleeting moment . . . when he had but a mere seventy-two hours to live.

As we left the Carlyle in an SS/BOSSI motorcade to bring him to the airport, we were working under unusual JFK staff orders. There was be to no NYPD motorcycle presence, and we were to stop at all appropriate traffic lights. Since it was a private visit, that tact was an apparent attempt to negate the inevitable crowds caused by a normal presidential motorcade.

That did not work when we stopped at 57th Street and Fifth Avenue. Someone spotted him in his limo, and before the two-minute light changed, there were at least twenty people yelling and waving at him. We had to exit our follow-up vehicles, not because it was necessarily a security problem, rather, to contain their enthusiasm. Smart guys in the VIP security business know that, in most cases, the best security is an unplanned surprise move by a subject.

The ultimate irony of that story is that the same White House staffers overruled the Secret Service when they wanted to put a protective "bubble top" on Kennedy's Dallas limousine. Their reasoning was due to implied threats on Kennedy's life by a small group of right wing "nuts" in that city. A local newspaper ad, which ran on the day of his assassination, suggesting he was a traitor to the United States indicated of that type of thinking.

Lee Harvey Oswald was not a right wing nut, rather, a left wing psychotic, who, just prior to the assassination, was the self-announced leader of the pro-Castro Fair Play for Cuba Committee's New Orleans chapter. Subsequent inquiry revealed the "chapter" had but one member—Oswald.

I had been investigating the parent group (based in Manhattan) along with the FBI for about five years. When it surfaced in a televised news flash about the assassination that he was an FPCC member, I threw a glass against the wall of my BOSSI office in anger, wondering at that moment, if somehow we missed a chance to surface his New Orleans activities prior to his Dallas madness; fortunately we did not.

There is a cornucopia of never-ending conspiracy theories about JFK's assassination. As one who frequently had the experience of checking out surprisingly numerous threats to the various presidents/vice presidents that came into the city for visits, I came to know the nature and pattern of most all of those suspected in that way out activity. With hardly an exception, they were all brooding, psychotic loners seeking some kind of weird personal aggrandizement.

Oswald more than fits the classic psycho pattern I ran into. The only difference between Oswald and those I investigated was that he succeeded by the purest form of statistical chance without financial help, logistical support, or direction from anyone. My guys only dreamed about that.

As far as I am concerned, Oswald was not, in any way, conspiratorially tied (in the months and weeks before the assassination) to the Italian mob, the Soviet KGB, Fidel Castro, Jack Ruby, Howard Hunt, or anyone else. Why is that? Simply because this is very strong evidence to the contrary.

On April 10, 1963, seven months prior to Kennedy's assassination, he attempted, but failed, to assassinate right-wing U.S. Army General Edwin Walker at his Dallas residence by firing one rifle shot through Walker's dining room window. Investigation showed that Walker survived that attempt only because the bullet struck the wooden frame of the window, thereby deflecting its path. I therefore submit: here was a left-wing psycho trying to kill a right-wing leader.

The rifle he used was the same Mannlicher-Carcano type rifle found near his sniper's location on the sixth floor of the Dallas School Book Depository. Note below the now-famous Oswald photograph with the rifle in hand outside his Dallas residence.

Responsible investigators curl their lip at conspiracy theorists who suggest/believe/hope the original photo was altered by having Oswald's face superimposed (whoopee!).

If one wants to know exactly where that bogus theory began, go no further than Oswald's interrogation by Dallas and federal authorities. They dramatically handed him the damning photo. He responded by stating that it was not him, someone had superimposed his face in the photo. Thus, another million-dollar conspiracy rip-off was born.

Much more damning is the later testimony of his wife, Marina. She flatly affirmed that she took that photograph of her husband, along with strong supporting testimony affirming his detailed movements and activities prior to and after that Walker assassination attempt.

She also provided investigators a most damning document, secretly hidden and written in Oswald's hand, which was his "assassination diary," if you will, which detailed solitary surveillance activities at the Walker residence, along with escape routes to be utilized after the deed was done.

Another conspiracy putdown is that the one rifle bullet used in the Walker attempt has been proven (by sophisticated neutron-activation tests) to come from the very same manufacturer of the bullets as the ones that killed Kennedy.

Further, and I believe most important of all, is that there is a documented letter that Oswald wrote to a Communist Party member indicating that he attended an "ultra right" (Oswald's words, folks) meeting in Dallas, headed by General Walker on October 23, 1963.

That meeting was six months after his Walker assassination attempt, but, critically, just thirty days prior to Kennedy's assassination. In my opinion, that document strongly indicates that Oswald was STILL morbidly focused on Walker at that late moment.

Thus, any reasonable person could assume that he was not then running around, compiling a new and/or concurrent "assassination diary" for the JFK hit with any one of five or more alleged co-conspirator entities (take your pick). Indeed, there does not exist, in the public record or elsewhere, even a single credible hint that he ever acted with any other person in any Kennedy assassination plot.

(Note: The above has been my contention for a number of years. Vincent Bugliosi's recent best seller, *Reclaiming History*, covering just about every angle on the assassination, stresses that same point, perhaps more than any other.)

It is most salient, too, that Oswald, on precisely that date, had not a clue on the yet-to-be publicly announced Dallas motorcade route of the president. Why? Because that decision was still under consideration by motorcade planers and Kennedy staff. In fact, two others were then under serious consideration by JFK advance men and the U.S. Secret Service. Check it out.

Thus, it could just as easily been a route other than the one that went past, the Texas School Book Depository. When that fateful announcement appeared in Dallas newspapers, there were but seventy-two hours to go before the motorcade event. Then, and only then, did Oswald learn the presidential motorcade would go directly by the building in which he worked.

That is, unless you are an Oliver Stone fan who might well surmise that: Maybe, just maybe, there was a CIA plant in the Secret Service who was feeding Oswald constant information on the course of the motorcade route deliberations. Hmm . . . yeah . . . and maybe that "plant" was good enough to steer SS participants to the School Book Depository route, too . . . YEAH!

If you wish better information than my conspiracy denigrations here, I suggest that you watch the often-shown documentary on the History Channel. It is entitled, "The Kennedy Assassination-Beyond Conspiracy." I contend that it effectively destroys all of the so-called credible assassination theories, e.g. there is "proof" that a shot/s came from the "grassy knoll". . . er, wait a minute, the KGB did it; no, hold on, the Italian Mob did it, no, er . . . si!, Castro did it.

"No, no, the CIA did it," says Oliver Stone, whose JFK assassination film alleged there were three expert assassins in Dealey Plaza, firing not three but six shots at JFK (whew!). While it does not specifically address my above Walker motorcade-route observations, it does conclusively state (along with Bugliosi) at the end of its masterful presentation: "THERE WAS NOT A SINGLE PIECE OF EVIDENCE TO PROVE A CONSPIRACY."

Those who continue to try to profit from new and better conspiracy theories usually go mute or otherwise flimflam and change the subject when confronted with that program's factual revelations.

Me? I contend that political assassins the world over rarely, if ever, have gone around killing or attempting to kill both, right (Walker) and left (Kennedy) political figures. Unless, of course, the assassin were a prime candidate for a special room at New York's Bellevue Hospital for the mentally insane.

(A devastating, ironic note: on the morning of the assassination, before emplaning to Dallas from Houston, JFK advised his wife, "Today we are heading to 'nut' country.")

MY "nut" candidate is Lee Harvey Oswald, who, as an already troubled fifteen-year-old living then in the Bronx, rode New York's subways alone for hours and hours, undoubtedly passing by Bellevue; but as history shows, he never got off at that stop.

Anyway, on to other observations, much less sanguine. You never knew what you were going to see and hear on a security escort assignment. I was close by JFK and Eleanor Roosevelt when the former first lady was complaining to him about the traffic conditions, causing her late arrival at the Waldorf function. He smilingly counseled her saying, "Blame it on the Mayor, Eleanor."

When the huge crowd surrounding the Hotel Roosevelt, in the final moments of the 1960 Presidential campaign, prevented his tailor from delivering his suit prior to an important public rally that night, JFK exited his bedroom suite clad only in a towel. He evoked sailor language directed to his stunned aides, shouting, "Where the ------ is my suit!" Everyone ducked for cover, while NY cops ran and found the tailor, still struggling to enter the hotel.

Later that evening, I was standing next to him on the dais of the outdoor rally while he waited to speak to the overflow crowd. His namesake, Steve Kennedy, then NYPD Commissioner, was attempting, somewhat obtrusively and in animated fashion, to give him some type of NY political insight. JFK, while polite, was barely listening. His mind was on what he was going to say.

JFK's political league was the majors; Steve Kennedy's, the minors. Mine? Little league, but I occasionally do remember what politicians have said or done in my presence.

First Lady Jacquelyn Kennedy came to the city on a private visit on August 22, 1962. After she exited her plane at La Guardia airport's Marine Terminal, the *New York Daily News* photographer snapped a photo of her and me as she walked to her limo. When I saw the photo, I was annoyed with myself, for stupidly wearing a sports jacket instead of a suit. Apparently, I had not learned a lesson from Bob Bystricky; but at least I didn't say, "Right this way, Jackie."

My Secret Service partner on that assignment was Al Wong. He eventually became the secret service agent-in-charge of its Technical Services Division. I will have something interesting to say about me, Al, and the aforementioned Jack Ragan later on, in the Watergate chapter.

One final LBJ/Waldorf Astoria story (promise!). On October 21 of the 1968 presidential campaign, Nixon was in his Waldorf suite about to attend the annual Alfred E. Smith memorial dinner in the hotel's Grand Ballroom. The high profile charity function, always attended by the catholic elite of New York, was almost an attendance requirement for presidential candidates in an election year. In the 1960 campaign, Nixon and Kennedy were speakers at the function.

Both Nixon and Vice President Humphrey were invited and scheduled to speak by the then New York catholic archbishop, Terrence Cook, soon thereafter to become a cardinal. The presidential race, just weeks before the election, had tightened considerably, so the high profile dinner got super media attention. A strategic slip by either candidate could be very telling. Then the democrats opted to play hardball.

Less than two hours before the program was to begin, a Secret Service agent confidentially advised me that an additional guest, previously unannounced, was on his way to the dinner: President Lyndon Baines Johnson! The "two on one" move was unheard of in the annals of the Smith dinner history.

I quickly went up to the Nixon suite where he and Haldeman were meeting. I gave them both the hot-off-the-intelligence-press news. Their reactions were 180 degrees apart. Haldeman exploded, using street invective (I am being nice) to characterize his take on the democratic move; vetting what he felt was a political conspiracy (sorry) engineered by the archbishop in concert with LBJ for the benefit of Humphrey.

Nixon's reaction to both the news and Haldeman's outburst was surprisingly calm. I attribute that to his long experience attending that function as Vice President, as the 1960 candidate, and as a private citizen leading up to that election. He would know intuitively it was not who was there, rather, it was the impact of what was said within the strict allotted time constraints by the speaking guests.

Assuming he made that calculation, he was right, because Humphrey blew it by speaking for twenty minutes longer than his allotted time. That crowd was not only sophisticated, but in the tradition of the good governor, Alfred E. Smith (a strong opponent of prohibition), there was a time to talk and a time to drink; LBJ's presence notwithstanding.

Johnson's opponent in the 1964 presidential election was Senator Barry Goldwater, who came to the city in the early fall of that year for a fundraiser at the exclusive University Club in Manhattan. I was in his limo with him and his aides when we returned to his hotel at Central Park South.

As we approached, we spotted a small, pro-Goldwater demonstration in front of his hotel. To my surprise, he tapped me on my shoulder and said, "Jack is there any other entrance to my hotel?" I told him that there was not. He had no interest in meeting with those supporters, which, to my mind, said a lot about his election chances; perhaps contributing to his pretty good beating in that election.

On that same visit, I was in an elevator with him and an aide, who was telling him that a contributor wanted to meet with him. Goldwater, apparently annoyed, said, "I don't want to meet with him."

The aide, apparently not in agreement, said, "But, Barry, he has given us, $25,000." The candidate responded, as the elevator door opened, "Give it back to him." Hmm.

On the subject of money, I once filled in for the BOSSI detective, who had the NYC security detail for the then New York governor, Nelson Rockefeller. As I was taking him to his residence that evening, he said, "Detective Caulfield, I came out without any change, could I trouble you to get me a *New York Times* at that newsstand?"

As I was making the Rockefeller purchase, I chuckled at the irony of my mother's laughing reaction (when I was ten years old), to the big news that the Governor's grandfather, John D. Rockefeller, was altruistically giving away dimes to almost anyone he ran into. She had a good laugh, once again, when I told her MY Rockefeller story.

Chapter 3: The Near Assassination of Ernesto "Che" Guevera

I had two things in common with the late Che Guevara on December 11, 1964. One, we had Irish grandmothers and two, as I subsequently learned, we came close to simultaneously meeting our maker via a bizarre series of assassination attempts on his life in NYC on that date by three, more than capable, anti-Castro terrorists.

It was approximately 1:00 a.m. and I was having trouble sleeping at my Rockland County, New York residence. I knew I was in for a tension-filled day as an NYPD detective. I was then thirty-five years old and the department's pro- and anti-Cuban expert, assigned to the elite Bureau of Special Services and Investigations (BOSSI). I was also part of the BOSSI security team assigned to protect Guevara, who was then Cuba's "Minister of Industry" (an unlikely title). He was scheduled to address the United Nations General Assembly at noon that day.

When our department was notified a few weeks before by the State Department that he was coming to New York City, I became concerned--and with ample justification, because as soon as word of his visit was made public, the Cuban anti-Castro community in New York and Miami exploded in outrage. Guevara was no low-level Cuban diplomat about to be engaged in a perfunctory duty at the UN. To them, he epitomized the brutality of the Castro communist regime; he was reliably known to have personally reveled in and supervised the execution of many of Castro's enemies via firing squads over a brutal six-year period following the successful Castro revolution and the U.S. disaster at the Bay of Pigs in April 1961. Purportedly, such executions were continuing even as Guevara's visit to New York was announced.

Conversely, the American and international hard-left were delighted to have this most colorful revolutionary dreamer be given the ultimate international stage, the UN, as a platform to further their many radical causes worldwide. Couple all of this with Che's unquestionable romantic flair, accented by his black beret, good looks, and military uniform, it was fair to say that anything could happen and, as events quickly proved, it certainly did.

At that time, the NYPD was (and still is) the best police department in the world with regard to protecting controversial heads of state and notable international political figures. This was due primarily to the presence of the UN in New York where, sooner or later, most such figures either spoke at or otherwise visited. There is nothing quite like experience in the art of Head of State/VIP protection—the NYPD has it in spades.

Add the resources of men and material that the department can bring to bear on any controversial visit, and you have the absolute best protection that can be offered any figure; even a guy like Che Guevara. Having said that, I am quick to point out that the absolute perfect record of the BOSSI unit in the area of VIP protection, notwithstanding such experience and resources, has a lot to do with sheer luck and circumstance. One doesn't have to go beyond the assassination in Dallas to see that two or less seconds either way in that tragic motorcade could have aborted John Kennedy's assassination. As I will show, quick momentary decisions on the part of the terrorists (along with perhaps the Irish luck of both my grandmother and Guevara's) changed the subsequent assassination attempt on his life via a timed bazooka shelling from two prospective locations in Manhattan, to a location directly opposite the rear of the UN building on the then-desolate Long Island City side of the East River. The device was hastily assembled there by three anti-Castro terrorists in the wee hours of that morning, and set to fire at the UN building automatically at 12:10 p.m.—the same moment that Guevara was speaking to the General Assembly.

The previous day, the NYPD BOSSI team, along with State Department security agents, with whom we then jointly worked on such assignments, was able to get Guevara and his entourage to the Cuban Mission to the UN (located at 6 East 76th Street, Manhattan) from the airport without incident. But we were struck by the hugely vociferous anti-Castro, anti-Guevara demonstration at the airport and also in the contained area near the Cuban

Mission, just 100 yards from Fifth Avenue and Central Park. Guevara had elected to use the Mission as his headquarters for his stay in New York. High security was in effect at both ends of the 76 Street block and was tightly sealed by uniformed police and detailed detectives—so far so good.

But security concerns were growing exponentially as threats flowed into BOSSI via U.S. intelligence agencies, literally from around the world. Such threats to visiting controversial figures were nothing new to BOSSI. While most were often meaningless, they made us ever mindful that we were always engaged in hazardous work. But the "decibel level" on this assignment was far different. The intensity of the Guevara threats surpassed even those we had experienced during the NYC visits of Fidel Castro in 1959 and 1960. At that time, Castro had not officially aligned himself with the Soviet bloc, the Bay of Pigs invasion was still to come, and the Soviet intercontinental ballistic missiles were yet to be planned for assembly ninety miles from the United States mainland. Further, in 1960 the sadistic execution of Castro's Cuban enemies was only being hinted at publicly. Therefore Fidel's vulnerability, while serious, was not as great as Guevara's in 1964.

As soon as we learned that Guevara was to remain at the Cuban Mission for the night and his next move was to the UN for his speech at noon the next day, the day detail of uniformed police and local squad detectives was turned over to the night time detail. It was now 1:30 a.m., and I still couldn't get to sleep. At about that moment, the beginning of three insane planning sessions to assassinate Guevara began in Manhattan. The three anti-Castro terrorists, Ignacio and Humberto Novo (brothers), and Julio Perez were attempting to enter the block where the Cuban Mission was housed. All three were known to me (via my investigation of both pro- and anti-Castro groups in NYC) as members of the small New York chapter of the Miami-headquartered Cuban Nationalist Association. The FBI had identified the parent group as possibly the most violence-prone of all the anti-Castro groups in the United States. They also had confidentially advised me that the Miami group was highly suspect in the blowing up of a Cuban freighter in Montreal Harbor, some ninety days before Guevara arrived in NYC.

My office had thus begun to pay NY-CNA members a lot of attention, determining they were closely associated with an American anti-Castro gunrunner, married to a Cuban. That fact became salient later on in our investigation. But we had no prior information, nor did the FBI, that they were plotting the assassination of Guevara. Of course, once his visit was formally announced, we put them on our close watch list, seeking to determine if they were going to sponsor demonstrations or engage in any conduct we considered worthy of further investigation. We found nothing unusual other than the likelihood they would engage in some sort of demonstration during the Guevara visit. It turned out to be more than just a demonstration!

As we later surprisingly learned, the reconnaissance entry into East 76th Street by the three terrorists was to see if it was possible to enter the tenement directly opposite the Cuban Mission, journey to the top windowed landing, and there assess the potential to reassemble Perez's bazooka device and automatic timer (placed in the trunk of his vehicle, a block away from the Cuban Mission). The idea was diabolical, yet simple. If that could be accomplished, the time of Guevara's departure later that morning for the UN would be estimated, the timing mechanism would be set, and with luck they would become the heroes of the anti-Castro movement worldwide.

Of course, had they been successful, I possibly wouldn't be writing this because when assigned to a BOSSI security escort, you were required to stand near the subject's vehicle until he enters; then you quickly enter yours and the motorcade begins. Actually, the mathematical odds of a bazooka detonation killing him at the precise moment of his departure from the Mission made it statistically improbable that their assassination attempt would have been successful. But with my partners and myself all waiting in the vicinity of Guevara's limousine, the threat to us was far greater than Guevara's.

In any event, the roll of Irish-Luck began when the terrorists were challenged by a uniformed cop on duty in the block (where Guevara was then sleeping). I still don't know who that officer was. If by some chance he reads this account I would like to speak to him and thank him profusely. The terrorists obviously gave the cop an acceptable cover story, and inasmuch as they weren't carrying the bazooka, he merely chased them from the block.

Emboldened by that encounter, they then brazenly journeyed around the block and quietly entered Central Park on foot to a point behind a huge rock (still there today) that was directly opposite and about 100 yards from the Fifth Avenue entrance to 76th Street, where the Cuban Mission was located. Julio Perez, the bazooka technician on the team, then had the sole call. Could he set up the bazooka device behind the rock, and get the proper trajectory to have the shell detonate in front of the Cuban Mission at the estimated time of Guevara's departure for the UN? Perez was no technical lightweight. A bazooka operator in the Bay of Pigs invasion, he was employed in Manhattan as a teletype repairman. Again our luck held, after analysis Perez said no to his co-conspirators—the angle would not permit an accurate detonation from that relatively short distance.

Thus the terrorists, still focused and determined, next motored to a desolate location at the water's edge on the Long Island City side of the East River, directly opposite the UN building. Perez then went to work in earnest. He began to assemble the bazooka with its timing device on an ordinary milk crate and, looking at the omnipresent UN building, began his trajectory calculations. It was approximately 3:00 a.m. For many who would journey to work at, or otherwise visit, the UN later that morning, Perez then made what turned out to be a most fortuitous error.

He calculated that the bazooka tube was too long and the shell would thus explode high above where he and his co-conspirators believed the General Assembly Hall was located. It was evident to me in reviewing the crime scene later that for the shell to even have a remote chance to detonate in the General Assembly, it would have had to traverse through walls as well as the employees' cafeteria—a highly unlikely event. They were obviously groping in the dark; however, had the shell landed where Perez thought it would, the many UN employees and visitors having lunch at the time of the detonation most likely would have been victims of a horrible crime. Perez, with obsessive determination, thus proceeded to saw off twelve inches of the bazooka tube, insanely believing that such calculation would bring the shell right to the podium where Guevara was going to speak. He set the timing mechanism for 12:10 p.m., which was the only thing the terrorists got right. At the moment the shell did explode (100 yards short of the UN building in the water); Guevara was in fact addressing the packed UN assembly hall.

Amazingly, we later learned, Perez, taking a lunch break from his day-job repairman duties had proceeded to a point just a few yards south of the UN building in Manhattan, where he actually watched the shell fire from Long Island City and fall short into the East River, just shy of his target. There have been many fireworks shows in and around NY Harbor, but I venture to say none was weirder or potentially more deadly than that one.

It would be nice to write that the above fascinatingly accurate detail was independently uncovered by the detective/FBI investigation and/or admitted to by the terrorist themselves. Neither is the case. But a very sharp detective in the 17th detective squad, which covers the UN location, cleverly elicited this piece of information from none other than a cousin of the described Novo brothers! Below is a dramatic account of that squad interview.

Eight days after the shelling, the Novo cousin walked into the 17th Precinct Station House and headed for the detective squad office upstairs. He sat down and in a conspiratorial tone indicated to the detective that he had the complete details of the bazooka shelling of the UN. The detective did a double blink. The cousin went on to say he had just learned those details, in confidence, from a clandestine meeting with the three terrorists, two of whom were his cousins. He quickly added he had a quid pro quo for wanting to give up both his cousins and Perez.

The detective, suppressing amazement at what he was being told, expressed interest by saying, "Well, what do you have in mind?" (He was expecting an outrageous monetary figure). The now hyper cousin conspiratorially leaned over from his seat and said in a whisper, "All I want for my information is that you make me a cop!" The detective's first thought was to check and see if this guy just escaped from an insane asylum but, of course, New York is New York and he had seen and heard it all as a squad detective in Manhattan. He figured, "Let me go along with this insanity to see where it leads." With authoritative calmness, he then said, "Sure, guy, no problem, I'll take care of you; now slowly, so I understand, give me the details that you claim you have."

Without a moment's further hesitation, the cousin unloaded one of the more remarkable informer stories in NYPD history. Before the cousin had gotten too far, the detective, unaware of all of the above described information being generated by the Queens-based investigation, began to suspect that this cousin's madness might just be for real. Frankly, if the cousin had said that to me I would have gone one better; I would have skipped patrolman and offered to make him a sergeant!

The above non-fairy tale gets a little ahead of my involvement in actually getting all three terrorists to come in, confess, and thereby solve and close the case. It's one thing to receive information of this type from an unstable witness telling you a truthful story; it's another to force the participants to publically confess to a crime that was on the front pages of just about every newspaper in the world. So let's go back to Che's UN visit.

At about 11:00 a.m. that morning, the Guevara security detail in front of the Cuban Mission was ready to go via motorcade to the UN. Proforma, my partners and I were standing at Guevara's vehicle waiting for his exit from the Mission. Out he came wearing his signature black beret and military fatigues, the same type worn by Castro some four years earlier on his visit to the UN. I noticed he was in a lighthearted mood, chatting with Cuban UN officials and some hard-eyed Cuban security people. All of a sudden I realized that I had become the object of his smiling demeanor. He nudged one of his aides and, apparently speaking about me, got a good laugh, from his subordinates. It took me a few seconds to figure out what the joke was and then I realized he was mesmerized by the dopey looking, pork-pie hat I was wearing that day. To Guevara, I must have looked like a caricature of the "gringo" American security agent he surely must have heard so much about during the course of his lifelong political intrigues. With tongue in cheek, I smiled back at Guevara, resisting the temptation to loudly comment to my colleagues on Che's equally outrageous black beret. Little did either of us realize that only ten hours earlier an attempt was made to blow Guevara and his entourage to bits at this very spot.

The motorcade, guided by the always-talented NYPD motorcycle men, efficiently took off on a prearranged diversionary route, heading directly east to the East River Drive, as opposed to south to 42nd Street, and entering the UN at the main First Avenue entrance—where we knew a massive demonstration of anti-Castro Cubans was waiting to vent their rage (or worse) as the motorcade passed. I vividly recalled that during the 1960 visit of Castro to the UN; his motorcade did enter the UN from the main First Avenue entrance. Just as his motorcade was passing anti-Castro demonstrators in a designated demonstration location, a wide-eyed Cuban with a box in his hand broke through the police barrier and on a dead run, threw the box at Castro's vehicle. I was in the BOSSI vehicle directly behind Castro's limo, guns quickly came out of holsters, but too late; the box hit the side of Castro's vehicle. The sigh of relief was palpable to all as the box opened and three white doves flew out, harmlessly. Nervous laughs didn't hide the reality of the dangerous business we were in.

But this time we were not going to give the anti-Castro/Guevara demonstrators a similar opportunity. Hence, we chose the diversionary route. We would enter the UN from the close-by East River Drive exit and then scoot a short distance directly into the employees' basement entrance where, in concert with UN Security, risk of a security mishap was minimal. Once we got into the UN building I relaxed because UN Security took over and I believed we had nothing to do until his departure, a few hours hence. But I was quite wrong ... nearly dead wrong!

At 12:10 p.m. the bazooka shell detonated from the LIC shoreline and traversed about 900 yards toward the looming UN building. It hit, into the East River, with a loud explosion just 100 yards from its intended target. I was in an alcove at the UN's General Assembly Hall, not far from where Guevara would exit when he finished his speech. An enraptured delegate audience, many from the underdeveloped countries (an ideal constituency for Che), hung on his every word. I happened at that moment to be looking at the U.S. Ambassador to the UN, Adlai Stevenson. He was looking at Guevara, holding his eyeglasses in his hand. At the sound of the terrific explosion, he dropped his glasses on his delegate's desk in shock. Simultaneously, the rest of the delegates reacted either in a loud exclamation or involuntary movement, some panicked towards the exits.

My instant reaction was to see if Guevara was hurt in any way. Apparently he wasn't. Coolly, with only a minimal hesitation, he resumed his speech. I knew that while at the UN, we, the NYPD, had no jurisdiction over the protection of Guevara. Besides, the UN security staff instantly moved to the podium, in a protective move. But, for all anybody knew at that moment, the explosion could have merely been a prelude to a wide-open terrorist attack from the street, similar to the Puerto Rican Nationalist terrorist shooting of the U.S. Congress back in the 1950s. That was my immediate concern.

As best as I could determine at that moment, the explosive sound came from the front of the UN building on First Avenue. I headed there on a dead run, hitting the street no more than forty-five seconds after the explosion. What I saw was chaos. The thousands of anti-Guevara demonstrators effectively contained in the demonstration area opposite the UN had, in reaction to the explosion, broken police lines and were careening about in total confusion with NYPD mounted and uniformed police trying to contain them. I ran up to the nearest NYPD superior officer, a captain, and said, "Where the hell did the explosion come from?" I could see no signs of an explosion or any injuries.

He said, "No, the explosion came from the other side of the UN building." Another dead run and the first phone I could get to in the UN building, With my mind on fast-forward I called Manhattan police headquarters, told them it was an emergency and to put me through forthwith to the NYPD Harbor Precinct, which was responsible for patrolling the waters around the city and was on UN duty that day. Identifying myself, I said, "We've heard an explosion behind the UN building, have your patrol boats seen or can they verify anything?"

The answer was quick and to the point. "Yes, one of our boats has just reported an explosion in the East River about 100 yards from the UN building. They think the explosion came from the Long Island City side of the river and they are heading over to check it out. "

That was all I needed. I broke the connection and called my office, getting on the line with Lt. Barney Mulligan, one of the BOSSI superiors. I said, "Lieutenant, we've just had an explosion in the East River, about 100 yards from the UN building. This has got to be anti-Castro related. I suggest you pull the file on the New York arm of the Cuban Nationalist Association (CNA)." Confused at the request, he asked why. I said, "The bureau (FBI) has previously advised me that the CNA parent group, out of Miami, blew up a ship in Montreal harbor about ninety days ago. The New York arm of that organization is just as crazy. They are capable of something like this. As we speak, Lt., that group would be my top-of-the-head choice."

I guess everyone has a defining moment in their career, and this was mine, for after seven years of intensive work on the Cuban case, I knew it very well. The educated guess I took at that time was right on the money—ten days later I personally arrested the Novo brothers and Perez for the crime. They came to admit their guilt quite reluctantly, as we shall see. Photographs of their formal booking appeared on the front page of most newspapers throughout the country, if not the world. I was right there beside them. As a detective, it never got any better than that.

Within an hour of the explosion, local squad detectives and their bosses descended on the crime scene at the water's edge, examining the bazooka, timing device, milk crate, etc. It was clear to all that this was anti-Castro, related to the Guevara visit. The bosses, conferring with the Chief of Detectives and superiors at BOSSI, quickly realized that someone in the department with knowledge of anti-Castro elements in the city was going to have to assist the local squad detectives, who had little or no experience in matters of this type. Resultantly, BOSSI boss Bill Knapp called and told me I was being immediately taken off the Guevara detail, I was to report forthwith to the 108th Squad and give all the assistance I could in helping solve the case.

On my way to the 108th Squad, which covered Long Island City and therefore had jurisdiction over the investigation, I foresaw the turf problems I would encounter with this assignment. While this was a local crime, it clearly had national and international ramifications. Indeed, within a few hours of the intensive investigation, my FBI sources advised me that President Lyndon Johnson was already on the phone with New York Mayor Robert Wagner, telling him of his outrage and that he wanted this case solved, quickly. No doubt J. Edgar Hoover had received a similar call from LBJ.

The problem in those days was that whenever there was a major case with overlapping jurisdictions in major crimes, such as auto theft rings or bank robbery, Hoover invariably tried to posture his bureau in the best light and cut out the local police. So there was an innate suspicion that existed at the local squad level regarding working cooperatively with the FBI. But this animosity did not exist within the BOSSI unit. The investigative work of both entities regarding terrorist or extremist groups needed their combined expertise and resources to be effective. Additionally, the FBI had the foresight to have their able agent, Gus Micek, function as daily liaison with BOSSI. The information we were able to provide the FBI via that channel, certainly made their work in NYC much easier. It was a very effective arrangement because BOSSI received, in return, access to most of the appropriate FBI files and resources regarding our NYPD investigatory responsibilities.

But I took it a step further with regard to my Cuban assignment. The NY office of the FBI had one Francis O'Brien as my counterpart. O'Brien turned out to be the best on-the-street intelligence agent in the entire federal establishment with regard to the Castro government and its intentions worldwide. He was truly an amazing man with an unbelievable memory for names, dates, and almost any fact having to do with the Cuban revolution. Indeed, O'Brien was the only American agent ever mentioned publicly by Castro as being an enemy of his revolution. He was quite right. Over the many years of working with O'Brien, I became privy to much of his stunning trove of pro- and anti-Castro information. We also became very close friends. Recently, I learned he is seriously ill. I wish him only the very best. In my view, he deserves every accolade this government can bestow.

In preparation for my briefing to the detective superiors handling the case, I first called O'Brien who had previously informed me about the Miami-CNA's involvement in blowing up the Cuban freighter in Montreal. While he totally agreed with me that they should be a top candidate for the bazooka shelling, at that moment he had no direct information through his voluminous sources that they did. We both agreed that if this act originated with the large CNA group in Miami, the chance of a subsequent leak to the bureau was better. Lacking that information, we both speculated that possibly the very small NYC cell of the CNA might have been moonlighting independently. If so, this would make our task more difficult—for we were talking only about eight to ten active members and we had no way of knowing how they interacted with the parent CNA group.

In any event, I went into Queens County detective briefing first describing the relatively comprehensive monitoring of the anti-Castro groups by the BOSSI unit and my active seven-year role in that effort. Describing the cooperative Cuban case arrangements between BOSSI and the FBI, I could immediately sense that inherent friction that existed between the NYPD detectives and the FBI. I attempted to counter those attitudes by focusing on my long-term relationship with O'Brien, making a strong point that he was always open and above-board with me, and following that up with the contention that without FBI cooperation outside the city limits, we might have a tough time making this case. I wasn't sure I had convinced anyone at that meeting, but I knew I was right and was eventually proved so. I then quickly got into my educated guess about the CNA, citing the Montreal explosion in August and O'Brien's information that they were the FBI's prime suspects in that crime. That made a lot of sense to the bosses, so the order was quickly given to bring in the known NY-CNA members, which included the Novo brothers and Perez.

We first raided their one-room headquarters on the upper West Side of Manhattan and found nothing incriminating. Our interrogation of them in the 108th detective squad got nowhere, as well. They all had alibis as to where they were at the time of the actual shelling. We had no way of knowing then at what precise time they set up their device at the water's edge in LIC earlier that morning. Perez, I recall, stated that he was dutifully at work when the shell was fired. He obviously omitted where he was on his lunch break at the moment of detonation. I did note, however, that of all the others, Perez was quite intense, cold, and determined. That demeanor told me this guy might well be capable of killing a political enemy.

Having nothing but suspicions as to their involvement, we had to let them go. They were smirking as they left and I'm sure believed they had beaten the crime. I was disappointed but I should have known better, for things are never that easy; so I settled in for what I now knew was going to be a tough, hard-nosed investigation. I began supplying the detective investigators with other details I had on the Perez group, as well as other information on anti-Castro gunrunning activity that emanated in the City but had tentacles across the country. Generally we got nowhere, even with the implied threats of an immigration investigation—revolutionary Cubans always feared the green card. After about eight days of this, frustration began to set in and I sensed that the Department's "Cuban expert" was becoming less so in the eyes of my detective bosses.

Throughout this time I was in daily contact with O'Brien. He never wavered from his belief that the CNA was involved. Nothing that flowed into the FBI from their worldwide anti-Castro sources indicated other strong candidates for complicity. His steadfastness kept me focusing on the NY-CNA group. The American gunrunner, with the Cuban wife I mentioned earlier, became a serious focus of mine. He, I learned, was close to the Novo brothers, so I brought him in and got a commitment from him to transmit messages directly to the Novo brothers, if I so chose. He also had a federal firearms license, so I had the leverage to force this back-channel option. I took the chance that they might just want to contact me in this manner, too.

At about this time it became clear that the NY-CNA members we suspected needed a fear greater than jail if they were going to admit their complicity in the crime. I began to feel O'Brien out on any thoughts he might have in that regard. As we began brainstorming, I dropped the name of Rolando Masferrer Rojas as the one guy who might be able to pressure them to come in and confess. O'Brien knew exactly what I was talking about, for he had followed the activities of Masferrer closer than any other anti-Castro Cuban.

Masferrer was unquestionably Fidel Castro's most dangerous political enemy. A graduate of the same law school in Cuba as Fidel, he was as ruthless a foe on the right as Fidel was on the left. During the Cuban revolution, Masferrer, tied to the Batista regime, conscripted his own army of 2,000 men and went into the Oriente Mountains where Castro was headquartered and made every attempt to kill him. He failed, and by a whisker was able to flee Cuba hours before the overthrow in 1959. He had the well-earned nickname of "El Tigre" (the tiger) and O'Brien believed there was little he wouldn't do to kill or otherwise unseat Castro from power. Certainly, the Castro feeling was mutual. For sure, I wouldn't want to be the salesman who sold life insurance to Rolando Masferrer.

Rolando was then living in New York. Besides being ruthless, he was also brilliant. He had risen to be an editor of *La Prensa*, then the leading Spanish language daily in the city. From that vantage point he frequently took strong verbal potshots at Fidel. But in reality, O'Brien advised, this was merely a clever cover for his more sinister revolutionary anti-Castro activities. Also, he had the Cuban charm and good looks of his enemy, Fidel. Actually, you couldn't help but like the guy.

At just about the same time that O'Brien and I were discussing the use of "El Tigre" to force the CNA to admit their guilt, the bombshell report from the 17th Squad about the new "appointee" to the force, "Patrolman Cousin Novo," arrived at the 108th Squad. On the one hand, it was a stunning confirmation of my educated guess five minutes after the explosion; but on the other, I realized how close I had come to death. Those implications have never left me, even to this day.

Now the brainstorming sessions I had been having with O'Brien about Masferrer took on expeditious significance. I said to O'Brien, "Frank, what can you give me that will force Rolando to enthusiastically join our team?" What he then told me in detail was information that, in retrospect, broke the case wide open and was an affirmation of how critical it is in matters of this type to have the FBI as a cooperative ally.

O'Brien laid it out clearly. He said, "Jack, in February of this year, Rolando, in clear violation of stringent U.S. immigration restrictions on travel, went to Haiti and met with both Haitian and Cuban anti-Castro revolutionaries there with a view towards audaciously planning a counter revolutionary, violent takeover of the Castro government. He doesn't know that we know, and that information with all the implications of possibly being deported by immigration will shock him."

I asked if there was anything else. He said, "Yes, we've learned that he keeps a loaded .45 automatic in his desk drawer for protection. The weapon is unregistered, subjecting him to a NYC Sullivan gun law violation."

"In other words," I said, "either he joins our team or he is off to the slammer and/or deportation."

O'Brien said, "You got it, Jack."

When I brought this critical information to the chiefs and detective superiors, they were understandably elated because they knew that in the final analysis, this type of leverage can solve tough cases. So the stage was set for a dramatic career interview. I was directed to quickly get a meeting with Masferrer at his *La Prensa* offices, accompanied by a 108th Squad detective, and give him the good news. Concurrently, one of the detective superiors decided that it would be a good idea that we forthwith obtain authorized wiretaps at both Masferrer's office and his residence. The idea was that if Masferrer decided to cooperate and called one of the CNA, we might have the ballgame.

The interview at Rolando's office was indeed memorable. At first he was relaxed and smiling, because having met Masferrer at Cuban anti-Castro rallies over the years, he knew I would be interested in his journalistic take on the shelling subject and that is the way I played it at the start of the interview. Then I began the hardball phase.

I said, "Rolando, we have decided that we are going to need your help in this matter."

Sensing I was coming at him, he tried to put me off by saying, "Of course I will help you in any way I can, but what can I possibly do?"

It was time to level him. I now turned on my most serious look and said, "Look, Rolando, we are in a very tough ballgame here. It has come to our attention that in February of this year you were in Haiti in violation of your immigration restrictions and you know what can happen if that information winds up at the U.S. Immigration Service. Further, we have it on good authority that you have a loaded .45 automatic in your desk drawer here, which, as you surely know, is a violation of NYC's Sullivan law."

I stopped to observe the bombshell's effect. His dark eyes began to widen as the impact of what I had just said sunk in. I decided to be cordial and make it easy on him to do our bidding. "Look, Commandante, I am just as much an anti-Castro guy as you are, but you surely know what type of pressures we have to operate under when this type of international publicity hits our department. Now I am aware that you know the Novo brothers and Julio Perez very well. We also know that they did the shelling, notwithstanding the fact that they have denied it to us. All we want from you is your influential intercession with them to come in and do the right thing. Our interest in the matters that I just spoke of will at that point cease."

So Rolando had his deal and he clearly knew we had him. I was impressed that he didn't, in any way, challenge my serious allegations. O'Brien's startling professional information was, as usual, right on the money. However, I wasn't quite prepared for his reaction. He was obviously seething and attempting to control a temper that I really didn't want to contemplate, for, after all, this guy was a known political killer.

He tilted his head to the right side and began to twirl his moustache, slowly, said, "Caulfield, give me a call tomorrow. I will see what I can do." But the look he gave me really said, you are a son of a bitch and under different circumstances, I would kill you. Ignoring the killer look, I abruptly ended the interview figuring we had accomplished the purpose of the meeting and that the CNA was going to at least get the shit scared out of them. There would be no smirking now. And, we might just get lucky.

Rolando, too smart to call the CNA from his office, correctly figuring a wiretap, subsequently hurried to his home in Queens, where our second wiretap waited. Interestingly, Masferrer lived in the very same building the basement-alley where Kitty Genovese was murdered years before. The nearby public had ignored her loud, desperate pleas for help, as she slowly died. Her ignominious death was covered by the national media at that time.

Now high drama was to be added again to that infamous building. At about 6:00 p.m. on that evening, Rolando got Ignacio Novo on the phone from his residence. They obviously did know one another well from attending anti-Castro meetings and events in NYC. But not mincing words, Rolando, in high anger, got right to it in very colorful, street Spanish. He said, in part, "Listen to me shithead; I have much more important things to do than watch you and your asshole associates set off firecrackers in the East River. I had a visit today from Caulfield of the NYPD. Now, I am going to say this only once: you and your so-called revolutionary associates go in there and tell that son-of-a-bitch Caulfield what he wants to know or you will get a stick of dynamite up your ass. Do you understand?"

Ignacio understood alright. Nobody in the anti-Castro business could take a "suggestion" such as Rolando had just given and not comply forthwith. After a few pliant Si Sis from Ignacio, Masferrer, in apparent disgust, abruptly hung up the phone.

Ignacio then quickly contacted his brother and Julio Perez, and they then decided to communicate with me via the gunrunner previously mentioned as the back-channel contact. During the following day I heard from the now-exited gunrunner, advising me that the brothers Novo and Perez were considering surrender, but that Novo wanted to first talk with me personally at his job, which was at a shoe store on John Street in the city's financial district.

I met him there at about 8:00 p.m. He was sheepish and clearly shaken. Unhesitatingly, he indicated he wanted to surrender but asked for a potential deal-killer. He asked for a guarantee that he and his associates would not be charged with murder. Feigning strong annoyance, I quickly called the Assistant Queens District Attorney handling the case, put him on the phone with Ignacio and a verbal guarantee was given. It was as easy as that. Amazing what a threatened stick of dynamite from the right source can do for case-solving statistics!

Ignacio closed the shop and we were off to the 108th Precinct with siren blaring. By the time we arrived, a host of news reporters were waiting for us with cameras snapping everywhere. Up to the squad room we went while other detectives went out and rounded up Perez and Ignacio's brother. Inside of a couple of hours, I was standing at the 108th Precinct desk as the desk officer formally booked all three for the relatively minor crime of setting off an explosive device within city limits. As far as I was concerned, they lucked out; for it was clear to me that their intentions were to assassinate Guevara.

A month later at their formal court pleadings, an unusual event occurred. Their dapper American attorney arrogantly walked into the DA's office where all police concerned were assembled and introduced himself, passing out his business card as he went. I looked at the card and my eyes opened wide. The address of his law office was 120 Wall Street, Manhattan. There weren't many people outside of the CIA who knew that that was one of the addresses for CIA covert operations in New York City. I certainly did.

To say the least, the incident confounded me. Could it be possible that somehow the CIA sponsored this insane act of terrorism? The other troubling fact was that over time I learned that the parent CNA operation in Miami was reliably reported to have been on the CIA payroll. Lacking better evidence to the contrary, I believe that the attempted assassination of Guevara in NYC on December 12, 1964 was a loose-cannon operation by an uncontrolled arm of the parent organization, perhaps incited by the successful blowing up of the Cuban freighter in Montreal. It is likely that that operation was sanctioned by the CIA, and perhaps my NY crazies were just trying to emulate what they perceived to be a bigger and better thing, the assassination of Guevara in NYC.

In any event, looking back after all these years, it was certainly a seminal event—one I will never forget. The final footnotes to this tale are rather revealing. Rolando, predictably, never stopped in his single-minded pursuit of killing or otherwise unseating Castro. He had gotten into the drug business in order to finance his "revolution." When I wound up on the White House staff, he communicated with me from federal prison, seeking help to get out early. I sent a memo to John Dean, then counsel to the President and my boss at the time, indicating that properly handled by U.S. intelligence, Rolando could provide a valuable service to this nation in the never-ending clandestine war against the Castro regime. Nothing came of it. The last I ever heard of Rolando was in August 1971, some months after his communication with me. He started his vehicle on a Miami street and was instantly blown to pieces. Fidel's revolutionary league is certainly the majors. It appears Rolando lost, big time, in the playoffs.

As for Guevara, he, too, couldn't stop playing the game of intrigue. Revolution was literally his only bible and he kept at it in Africa, finally winding up trying to do a duplicate of Fidel's Cuban success in Bolivia in 1966. He failed miserably, and just before the Bolivian military executed him, (quite ironically) in a firing squad death, they interviewed him at length. It is reported that also attending Che's final interview was none other than the CIA station chief in Bolivia. Could that chief's presence be a damning confirmation of the CIA's long black interest (spells: assassination) in one of the most controversial figures of our time? I really don't know, but in that business, anything is possible.

Now, while long gone, Guevara is far from forgotten. He has risen from the ashes, if you will, to become a modern day icon to hard-left adherents worldwide. Books, documentaries, movies, and memorabilia abound. If I had been smarter, I could have had Guevara sign my dopey pork-pie hat. Auctioning it off today, I would use the proceeds to visit my grandmother's grave in Ireland, say thanks, and then give a "hooley" (a slam-bang, Irish party) for my relatives. Perhaps Guevara, now either looking up or down from his final resting place, and recalling his one-time humorous observation of my hat, might even approve.

Certainly, what can at least be said about Guevara and Masferrer via this story is that they epitomize that ancient adage, "If you live by the sword, you die by the sword." It remains to be seen how the now aging Fidel Castro ends his days. Time will tell if the adage will apply to him, as well.

Cuban security escorts and investigations understandably had BOSSI priority in the late fifties and early sixties. Aside from the inevitable assassination plots, gunrunning, etc. that emerged from visits of Cuban officials to the city during that period—the Che Guevara attempt being a good example—I ran into one in September 1962 that had a decidedly different twist.

I got a call at that time from an NYPD friend who, as a plainclothes cop, was working on gambling activities in "Da Bronx." He and his partners determined that the group they were focusing on got the bright idea to use a public pay phone as the main contact point for their not-so-nefarious activities. However, because it was a relatively large group of gamblers, they got permission to place a wiretap on that phone.

In his call to me, my friend said they heard foreign language conversations unrelated to gambling, but perhaps related to some type of Cuban and Haitian revolutionary activities (an aha moment?). Neither he nor his partner spoke Haitian and only limited Spanish. He knew that BOSSI detectives spoke various languages and wondered what we thought, because to them it sounded like maybe the Spanish end of the conversations involved a weapon shipment of some type.

He also said he and his partner learned that those using that phone rented a truck the day before from a business located directly across the street. They also determined that the Latino renters indicated to the owner that their destination was Miami, Florida.

We quickly got our hands on those telephone-taped bilingual conversations. Transcribing the Haitian language end was tough, because the language is a unique mixture of French and African patois. We sent the aforementioned French-speaking Frank Cresci to our UN contacts after he said he could not accurately translate it. That would take time, which we did not have; but the transcripts would be revealing later on in the investigation.

The Spanish end of the conversations was an eye-popper. It revealed that none other than the ubiquitous Cuban revolutionary, Rolando Masferrer, prominently mentioned in this book's Che chapter, was doing what came naturally: this time heading up a planned, armed invasion of Cuba from a Haitian coastal base, using Haitian conscripts in the United States, to enable that effort. The tapes also revealed that the truck destined to Florida apparently did contain a shipment of weapons, meant to further that cause.

Thirty-six hours had passed from the time we got the information indicating their Miami destination. We figured, in all likelihood, that we had missed the boat, if you will, and the so-called invasion force was already en route to Haiti.

Nevertheless, we notified the Florida state police, gave them the pertinent information they needed, and crossed out fingers. I am glad we did because heavenly intervention was with us, in the form of a hurricane sweeping through Florida at that fortuitous moment, considerably delaying all southbound traffic.

As the driver and passengers of our identified truck came across the Florida-Georgia state line, at 6:00 a.m. there was an alert Florida state trooper stationed there, and whoopee, he nailed the "revolutionairos" for us. His colleagues then found some $200,000 worth of weaponry in the truck; not exactly like the Normandy invasion.

But it was more than enough to satisfy the detective bosses, and get my Bronx, plainclothes friend a well-deserved pat on the back and a commendation, along with the BOSSI detectives working the case. Exhibiting cop humor when I told him he was getting a commendation, he said, "Hey Jack, do you think I should thank the bookmakers too?"

The priceless post-arrest chuckles we enjoyed came after our subsequent wiretaps were installed in an effort to get the complete picture on the so-called Cuban invasion participants. In the great tradition of Latin political conspiracy, the Cuban principals, e.g. Masferrer, out on bail were twirling their mustaches big-time, as they attempted to determine who, in their ranks was "el hombre malo" (no Spanish cusswords here!), or in Bronx parlance, "Which S.O.B. gave us up?"

Candidates abounded, as they went around and around like a dog chasing its tail. They never realized it was "A Bronx Tale" behind their failed mission.

Interestingly, when we translated the Haitian end of the tapes, we found a Haitian Roman Catholic priest participated in the plot. The tapes told us that his is interest in that "enterprise" was not so much the Cuban's aspirations, rather, the possible ouster of the terrorist Haitian regime of Francois "Papa Doc" Duvalier, known to be especially brutal to catholic clergy.

Reputed to be a cunning lunatic, he ruled the Haitian poor by permissively exploiting voodoo amongst them and used his secret police force, the infamous "Tontons Macoute," to repress all political and religious opposition.

I recall interviewing a one-time Castro official who had defected and was then engaged in anti-Castro activity in Manhattan. He told me that once, when on Castro's staff, he went on assignment to visit Papa Doc in his Port Au Prince palace, with the view towards improving Cuban-Haitian relations.

He brought with him a new, state-of-the-art camera he had just purchased, thinking that candid pictures of the meeting would be a good idea. As the meeting was moving along, but going nowhere, he realized that Papa Doc focused more on his camera than him.

Then through an interpreter, Papa Doc, made it clear that the only way the Cuban emissary was going to leave his palace alive, was to turn over his camera to him! Given the reputation of Papa Doc, he said, with tongue in cheek, "The 'diplomatic request,' was granted, instantly."

Ay Caramba might well have been the best Spanish words to describe that madness. Moreover, as history reveals, the Haitian equivalent of "All Rise" ever applying to Papa Doc Duvalier, in that or any criminal case, was but a mere voodoo dream.

Chapter 4: The 1968 Presidential Campaign

immediately began my duties with a Nixon trip to Atlanta; my first assignments. Returning to New York, I was accompanied by Nixon's wife, Pat Ryan Nixon. I found her to be an outstanding woman, reserved, but very alert and quite cordial. Frequently, in such security assignments, the security person must recommend techniques that sometime bear on the subject's privacy and convenience. Often, a wife doesn't appreciate or understand those necessary nuances. If not handled tactfully, problems of communication could develop. Thankfully, Pat Nixon did not, in any way, fall into that category.

At about 5:00 a.m. on the morning of June 5, 1968, I received a call from Bill Knapp, the BOSSI detective commander. He stated he had just received a call from the Secret Service that Bobby Kennedy was shot in California and that Lyndon Johnson had directed the Service to forthwith take over security for Richard Nixon. My first thought was, "There goes that assignment!"

I headed to the Nixon apartment on Fifth Avenue and met with Haldeman. I said, "Well, Bob, I guess my services are no longer required."

He called me aside and said, "No, on the contrary, I want you to take the position Chief of Staff Security for the Nixon Campaign beginning with the upcoming Republican Convention in Miami." (He certainly made my day!)

Then, a few days later, Nixon, the SS, and I attended the somber Bobby Kennedy funeral at St. Patrick's Cathedral, wherein Ted Kennedy gave a memorable eulogy.

Just prior to the convention, John Ehrlichman, the campaign director, called and said he wanted me to meet a the convention with a Jack Ragan, retired FBI wiretap expert, who provided his services to the Nixon law firm.

Jack, a small man with a smiling personality, had an outstanding FBI career, the most memorable of which was to create a bogus telecommunications system connected to the Soviet Mission to the UN on East 68th Street in Manhattan. In other words, every incoming and outgoing telephone call made from that location was monitored by the FBI! To those of us in that business, this was a happy surprise, hopefully ongoing today.

My conversation with Jack Ragan, given my inside view from a security perspective, was interesting, to say the least. I assisted Ragan in his duties, ensuring that the hotel rooms of key staff were checked and secured.

The introduction of unrelenting Miami heat made me yearn for upstate New York at that time of year.

The stunning announcement of Spiro Agnew to be Nixon's running mate, and the memorable acceptance speeches, were grandchildren stories, to be told.

Some Nixon advanceman got the idea for a "Nixon Navy," which was to party, with media cameras rolling, in front of the Fontainebleau Hotel, near the Miami Convention Hall. Don't know if the idea was worth it, but I could have made a few bucks selling anti-hangover medicine!

The Nixon strategists decided that, unmatchable, San Diego would be a great place to nail down all details of the forthcoming campaign, and so I was off to California for a glorious ten day "working vacation."

I hired the Wackenhut Security Company to secure the beachside complex, made it my business to get to know all of the key players, which would prove invaluable in the testing days ahead.

One night a group of staffers decided to "go slumming" in Tijuana, Mexico. I went along and whipped out my Spanish language qualification "card" and instantly became their tour guide. We wound up in a seedy bar, complete with Mexican hookers, one of whom offered cunelingus right from the top of the bar! Needless to say, business was brisk! I moved in front of the two female staff members attempting to shield them from the "free show." Of course, it didn't work, but at least the intent was there and, I was later told, appreciated.

As our gringo group left the bar, a swarthy Mexican made a nasty anti-American comment, picked up by myself and an associate, who also spoke Spanish. Suddenly, there was a head to head conversation between the gringo and the "revolutionairo," about the merits of communism versus capitalism in Mexican street-talk patois. Tones kept raising; it was time to go, forthwith!

And so the campaign began on Labor Day. We were to travel to seventy-seven cities in less than ninety days. The work was to be grueling. I became amazed at the stamina of Rose Woods, who had done that many times before.

I accidentally found her one morning at 3:00 a.m. typing to beat the band. Nixon was a lucky guy when he found her sixteen years before, a new Washington, D.C. arrival seeking work away from her hometown in Ohio. Not many knew she was a champion typist who could crank out ninety words per minute.

The assassination of Bobby Kennedy and Martin Luther King created a schism in the country, bordering on dangerous. The devastating anti-war riot at the Chicago convention left the hapless Hubert Humphrey in an untenable position, from which he could not recover, Lyndon Johnson, notwithstanding.

The Republican strategists were delights. But as far as I was concerned, it was a security wake-up call in that we were to be met in most cities by anti-war demonstrators; some were as virulent as their Chicago compatriots.

At one Ohio train stop, the rookie advanceman screwed up. Nixon was just a few yards from an almost out-of-control mob of about a hundred people. Incredibly, using the foulest of four letter words, they spat on him. I was stunned and simultaneously awed with his grit and courage; he spoke right past them, as if they weren't there. That video footage would certainly sell on eBay!

The Nixon team traveled on two private United jets, named the Julie and Tricia after his daughters. Occasionally, I traveled with the Secret Service in a more-than-slow Lear Jet. Many years later, it was alleged that Lyndon Johnson, exhibiting paranoia about a female Republican's contact with North Vietnamese negotiators, caused Nixon's plane to be bugged by the FBI.

I found the assertion humorous, in that the FBI official who was supposed to cause the wiretap was one, Deak Deloach, who had a onetime subordinate named Jack Ragan!

Back to the campaign. I had the presence of mind to photograph just about anything I thought might be of historical interest in the campaign. One of the most valued was getting my family in the foreground of a picture taken of Nixon speaking at a campaign rally in Long Island.

Another was one taken of me seated in Nixon campaign seat along with a Secret Service agent. He, a likable upstate New York Italian, also had a short fuse. He found the "hick" Secret Service supervisors demeaning and without a sense of humor (correct!). So to make a weird point, he tells me he decided to throw a supply of Nixon Security pins down a sewer drain one day in Pittsburgh! Don't know if that is true, but I do know I have campaign photos of the Pittsburgh campaign stop. (Madness!)

Somehow, I was able to get the Nixon Staff through the campaign without serious mishap. But, a couple of near misses come to mind. Jack Ragan, who was leapfrogging ahead of us on the campaign trail, discovered that prior to our arrival in Minneapolis, Wisconsin, Hubert Humphrey's home state; we learned he had been there just prior to our arrival. Sure enough, Ragan found someone (not a Nixon supporter) had placed wiretap equipment in the rooms we were to occupy. Se la vie!

Ehrlichman pulled me off the campaign trail to go in and supervise security for the upcoming live TV appearance from Madison Square Garden. He also asked me to brief seventy-five advance men on security procedures for the campaign. That night, a New York thief helped himself to the wallets of seven advance men. Ehrlichman had directed me that day to give them a lecture on campaign security procedures. Welcome to the Big Apple!

Governor George Wallace was also having a campaign rally at Madison Square Garden the week prior to Nixon's, so I went over to check it out from a security perspective. Two well-dressed blacks wearing ties came in. Within a minute, three redneck types were in front of them, mimicking a hanging and singing, "Yo' ain't gonna overcome in this place!"

The night of the Nixon rally, the advance men were trained and ready to go—until three Rabbis from Brooklyn attempted to enter the convention. One advance man from Iowa had never seen a Rabbi, and thinking they were hippies, attempted to deny them entry. I was beginning to think I was a fireman.

Despite our double screening the entrants, a wild-assed group of about a hundred anti-war hippies showed up early and got in before our process was in place. I summoned the Garden's President, Ned Irish, and said they had to go. He said he couldn't do that; I said I'll take care of it. I had hired ten off-duty cops for such a possibility, and they took good care of it, unceremoniously removing them as they yelled loud accusations of "police brutality," which were smilingly ignored.

The Madison Square Garden rally was to be Nixon's most important. Ed McDaniel, Nixon's longtime soundman fortuitously put in a redundant system because, believe it or not, a Democratic labor union pulled the plug just seconds before the speech began. We had lucked out.

Our final campaign stop was at the Century Plaza Hotel in Los Angeles. At a luncheon, Rose Woods approached me and told me that Nixon's nemesis, the incomparable Dick Tuck (who made history for causing Nixon's train to pull out as he was giving a speech), was gracing us with his presence. Uh oh—trouble in River City! I told Rose I would handle it.

At the event, I imposed upon a cute United stewardess. She loved the old man. I asked her if she would get Dick's attention and make him think he was the man of the hour. He was smiling as he left the room. For all I know, he might owe me one!

That, though, brings me back to the United Airline crew. One day, I was ahead of the boarding party and entered the cabin. To my shock, surprise, and humor, the entire crew was wearing oxygen masks, and it was no drill! Rather, they were using the masks as a rather unique way to quickly conquer hangover! Now, why didn't I think of that?

We were all near exhaustion as the campaign came to a close. I decided my presence was not necessary at the final rally in Los Angeles. So I watched it on TV with a key Nixon aide, the diminutive, brilliant Bryce Harlow, who was the first to see Nixon every morning on the campaign trail.

Nixon was going along pretty good when our eyes popped! He said in answer to an audience question, "Well when you come down to the nut cutting!" Harlow fell down on the bed, uttering the equivalent of "Oy Vey!" His shout reverberated down the hall.

But within an hour, the full-court press strategists were advising the giggling press that those memorable words were nothing more than famous New England slang. No one dared follow up on how Nixon knew that.

On the way back to New York for the campaign results, Nixon smiled at me and said, "Well, Jack, the hay is in the barn." Indeed it was.

I rushed home to vote before the long tension-filled night at the Waldorf Astoria, ending in euphoria and a hell of a celebration the following morning.

The key staff then assembled to plan for a new Nixon presidency. Shortly thereafter, Rose called and asked me to come down to the hotel. She told me she had just gotten a funny call from the daughter of a leading lawyer, whose firm was known to be the number one Democratic law firm. (I won't reveal that name here; the firm is too powerful and would be quite unhappy with the account below.)

In any event, Rose said the woman wanted to speak to a campaign official, because she has the keys to columnist Jack Anderson's office, where supposedly there was a valuable Nixon file! Haldeman, told me to go and see her in Washington, D.C., and find out what the hell she was talking about.

I met the woman at a restaurant. She, in my opinion, had a drinking problem. Without batting an eye as to the absurdity of the request she was making, she said she would turn over the keys for a mere $10,000.

I reported back to Haldeman, who said, "Meet here again and, in no uncertain terms, tell her it is no go, no way, no how!" We met this time in New York at a Park Avenue restaurant. To protect myself, I had three friends witness the conversation. Case closed.

When Haldeman gave me his marching orders, the soon-to-be-famous Henry Kissinger or, if you prefer, infamous, walked into the room and, not having any idea of who I was, offered Haldeman and John Ehrlichman, also present, daily security summaries he will be able to provide when he takes up his Assistant To The President For National Security Affairs duties at the White House. As soon as he left the room, Haldeman says to Ehrlichman, "The answer to that is no and we go from there." My first insight into big-time bureaucratic infighting!

After the campaign, John Ehrlichman called and asked what job I might like in the new Administration. I said, "I can make that one easy, John, the incumbent Chief U.S. Marshal is a former New York detective, put in there by Bobby Kennedy." Ehrlichman said that sounded good, advising me that he would tell John Mitchell, Nixon's former law partner, who also was the Campaign Manager. A Good guy, John, but he sure had a mind of his own, which caused him big-time problems, as we shall see.

A few days later, I was called by Ehrlichman who said John wanted to see me. His tone said my getting the job was a no-go. Mitchell tactfully tried to tell me why he couldn't support Ehrlichman's nomination. He said he had learned that the detective was about to be indicted for misappropriation of U.S. Marshall Funds. He died before that could occur. I said, "But John, I didn't take any money!" Precedent in that case, folded.

A couple of weeks later, Mitchell nominated an Army General, who with appropriate public fanfare, went through the nominating process. Mitchell wasn't smiling when it was discovered that the General owned a few unlicensed firearms! Another U.S. Marshal case closed.

And so, I had yet to land a job in the new Administration. It was already March, when Rose Woods walked into Ehrlichman's White House office and dropped a note on his desk that read, "What are YOU going to do for Jack Caulfield?"

My phone rang shortly thereafter, with Ehrlichman asking me if I would consider forming a security firm that would respond to requests for White House investigations. Taken aback, I said I would consider it and call him back in a few days. But, I had already made up my mind. To do so would endanger my police pension, because I was still on leave from the department.

When I called back, I gave him an alternative option: bring me into the White House and approve the hiring of an outside private detective—an NYPD detective—Anthony Ulasewicz, who was considering retirement. Two days later, the deal was done. I found myself having my photo take for my White House credentials. It was April 6, 1969.

My thoughts and tears turned to my father, the son of a dirt farmer in rural Ireland. We both cried the day I showed him my office and gave him a tour of the Oval Office.

God only knows what He has in store for any of us.

Chapter 5: The White House Experience

My multi-faceted, twelve-year BOSSI experience convinced me in late 1967 that Richard Nixon was going to run and likely win the Presidential election in 1968. I subsequently approached the Nixon people from the 1960 Presidential campaign (with whom I had worked as a BOSSI detective) and made it known I was available for candidate/staff security purposes during the 1968 campaign. I was interviewed and then brought on board by Bob Haldeman and Rosemary Woods as Chief of Security for the Nixon Campaign Staff.

That experience can only be described as one of the wildest, intelligence/security rides ever across America—in that it occurred within the anti-war, political-madness year of 1968. The assassinations of Martin Luther King and Robert Kennedy, along with burning cities and the anti-war riots at the Chicago Democratic convention and beyond were major contributing factors to what had become a nation in dangerous schism. Somehow, I got the Nixon campaign staff through associated anti-war campaign-turmoil occurring in a number of the seventy-seven cities visited by candidate Nixon without a security calamity.

But that successful effort was fraught with numerous misses, including a most memorable attempt at political sabotage by members of a democratic electrical union in NYC. They pulled the power plug, just as Nixon began his most important nationwide television campaign speech broadcast live from Madison Square Garden just days before the election. Fortunately, we had installed a redundant system, which was instantly activated. John Ehrlichman pulled me off the campaign trail to go into New York and supervise the security for that critical event—I had clearly lucked-out.

The Nixon victory thus led to my joining the White House Staff in April 1969 as Staff Assistant to the President, performing a dual role:

conducting discreet, wide-ranging investigations for the President and his senior staff. Simultaneously, I was engaged in multi-subject White House liaison activities (involving cross-border narcotics trafficking and monitoring violent anti-war demonstrations and events) with most of the leading federal law enforcement agencies, the White House representative at overseas Interpol conferences and the White House contact for the Agency for International Development's worldwide police support programs (essentially a CIA operation). Additionally, I was White House liaison with the National Association of Chiefs of Police.

Under my sole supervision, parts of these were field-investigated by Anthony Ulasewicz, the late, retired NYPD detective, whom I had arranged to be hired for that purpose. One such investigation ordered by the President included a discreet inquiry into Ted Kennedy's Chappaquiddick cover-up. (Ulazawicz would later attain his fifteen minutes of fame as a result of his Runyon-esque, highly humorous demeanor during his Watergate testimony).

My deal with Ehrlichman, regarding my employment, was that it was to be twofold. First, I would function as staff liaison with most of federal law enforcement, but primarily with the Secret Service, U.S. Customs, Interpol, and the International Association of Chiefs of Police. The government's focus on the anti-war movement and fledgling international terrorism all ensured that my days would go by quite quickly.

Second, via the Ehrlichman/Ulasewicz arrangement, I was to be the starting point for all investigations deemed necessary by the White House. Over a three-year period I was tasked with some ninety-three investigations, most in the mundane category, like why was the press making a big deal of Julie Nixon's new teaching job in Florida. Nobody but Nixon really cared. Seventy-three of those investigations became a part of Watergate history, when the "Waterfate" prosecutors became aware of Ulaswiecz's White House role in them, much to my disappointment and chagrin for him having done so without any notification to me.

The other investigations dealt with what was hot, from a White House perspective. Indeed, one day I looked at the front page of a newspaper and realized that on any given day, the White House was associated with some type of inquiry about the day's events, frequently resulting in my going to work, as opposed to spending time in the exclusive White House Health Facility.

I became close to Myles Ambrose, the colorful New Yorker who was the U.S. Customs Commissioner. I opened the White House doors for him; essentially closed to Rockefeller Republicans in the Nixon Administration. His social skills were something to behold and, resultantly, he showed me how to move and shake socially in the Washington scene that mattered a lot to some. It was almost a party a day. Great experience, but I quickly tired of the how-nice-to-see-you routine.

Indicative of the White House "bunker" atmosphere of that time were the over 300 82nd Airborne Division soldiers I observed in the basement cafeteria of the Old Executive Office Building (adjacent to the White House) on a Saturday morning in 1970. With bayonets fixed, they were a discreet reserve contingent ready to go if any of the 250,000, anti-war demonstrators outside broke through an ad-hoc barrier of over 300 commercial buses strategically placed bumper-to-bumper around the sixteen-acre White House complex. The idea was to prevent the "crazies" from jumping the White House fence. Intelligence sources indicated that that was the plan of a small way-out anti-war contingent. The strategy worked, although some of the more violent ones managed to nearly overturn one of the buses before being beaten off by Washington, D.C. police. In my mind, that event crystallized the White House's vulnerability to violently prone people.

Working at the White House is unlike any other governmental experience. Upon arriving at the White House for his National Security Advisor duties in 1969, Henry Kissinger remarked to John Ehrlichman, "Vere do we go from here, John?" He was right. I had a large office in that historic Old Executive Office Building, a secretary and White House mess privileges. In addition, a military chauffeur was at my disposal; super efficient White House telephone operators optionally placed calls that were always returned—and then there were the one-of-a kind Presidential trips on Air Force One. These trips were humorously highlighted by the traveling staff's betting pool that attempted to guess the exact time of arrival (anywhere), which was invariably within thirty seconds or less of the ETA.

A historically interesting event was the chance (there I go again!) White House-mess luncheon I had with then thirty-five-year-old Elvis Presley on December 21, 1970. This was just minutes after his famous visit with the President in the Oval Office. He sure was a country boy—right down to his grits side order. White House staffer Egil Krogh (also at the luncheon table) actually wrote an entire book on his visit! I didn't even have the presence of mind to get his autograph on the White House menu (the eventual value of which could have sent a grandchild to college).

Not in anyone's wildest speculation could it have been envisioned that I would, twenty years after joining the NYPD, become a public figure. That distinction resulted from the Watergate drama in which my investigative duties and other activities as White House Staff Assistant would, like dozens of my colleagues, come under intense review—and be laid out eventually in the public record. One of my post-White House activities fell into a controversial category, in that I was, in January 1973, unwittingly led by John Dean, then White House counsel, into the final moments of a disastrously imploding Watergate cover-up. I later learned that John Dean had silently masterminded the cover-up for six months. During part of my White House tenure, I had reported to Dean but I left the White House five months before the break-in and ensuing cover-up. Resultantly, I knew zero about Dean's cover-up activities—although it didn't take a rocket scientist to guess that something major was going on.

Only because my loyalty was to the president (no matter what the consequences), was Dean able to get my reluctant participation in arranging to obliquely transmit, via telephone, a fuzzily inferred Presidential commutation message to one of the Watergate burglars, James McCord. I initially believed that I was acting in the President's interests. As it turned out the entire matter accomplished absolutely nothing, but "trouble in River City." What I later shockingly learned was that not only was the message inane, but deceitful in that (as White House tapes prove) Nixon was in no way involved in, or had prior knowledge of that cunning transmittal.

In fact, the commutation message was arbitrarily composed out of thin air, in what was the most foolish of Dean's attempts to save himself during the last moments of his Machiavellian cover-up activities. John Ehrlichman had it about right when he publicly characterized Dean's action as "a monumental error." For his part, Dean masterfully avoided the entire matter in his book, *Blind Ambition*—oh, well.

He, thus, became my new boss; an event that I came to regret—for he was the historical catalyst for the termination of the Nixon Presidency. Each of us snared obliquely or directly in the Watergate net, had to go down our own road. He took the whistleblower road and has had to live with that decision, notwithstanding the strong caveat given to him by Fred Fielding, his closest assistant, at the critical decision-making time.

Chapter 6: Inside Watergate

As I sit down to write this chapter, I am struck by the magnitude of it all. Watergate was the greatest political scandal in the history of the country, if not the world, and I became enmeshed right on the fringes of it. (Whew!)

At last count, I identified at least a hundred books on the subject, seven of them by participants, all of whom went to jail.

I am the only person who knows precisely how and when it began. Shortly after I arrived at the White House, on April 6, 1969, I began examining how I might lend my knowledge of political security to the Republican National Committee. I received authorization from John Ehrlichman, then White House Counsel, to contact Barry Mountain, the Chief of Administration for the Committee. We talked, and both agreed a security capability was required, simply because it was nonexistent until then!

I reported back to Ehrlichman and got his permission to bring Jack Ragan, retired FBI and wiretap expert, on board for the security job. He had done outstanding work for us during the presidential campaign, leapfrogging ahead of the traveling campaign staff, electronically securing our hotel rooms before arrival. Further, I also advised John that we should include in his duties security for the then-fledgling Committee to Reelect the President (CREEP). He agreed, all was set in motion, and Jack began his security duties; all seemed to be going well.

On December 26, 1971, I received a disturbing phone call from Mountain. He said that at their Christmas Party, Ragan got embarrassingly drunk and fell to the floor in front of everyone (So did I when I heard it!). Mountain, in brisk, business-like terms flat-out said, "He has to go." I knew Jack liked his booze and did observe him under the influence on a few occasions; but he never exhibited a hint of loss of control.

I made it clear to Mountain that I was just as disturbed, but quickly bought a day to think about it, potential ramifications and all. When I called him back, I made a very spirited plea for my friend. But Mountain wasn't listening; and, unfortunately, it was his call, so the deed was done. Jack never called me about the matter, and I was glad about that.

Mountain then asked if I would find a replacement. I reached out to Al Wong, then the head of the Secret Service Technical Division, asking him to supply a list of Secret Service retirees who might fit the bill. I knew Wong from our joint NYPD/SS protective duties, when either or both the President and the First Lady visited New York.

(We spent a long evening on August 8, 1963 waiting for Jacqueline Kennedy to finish partying at an East Side bistro with her friend, an heir to the Spaulding fortune. Upon arrival, she and I were photographed at the airport, which was a front page photo in the *New York Daily News*. I wasn't dressed properly, I muttered to myself when I saw it.)

Wong, got back to me and said he had no Secret Service candidates, but provided me with the name of James McCord, who was retired CIA, previously in charge of their physical security division, which was salient to me in that the all-important criteria for the job was to ensure that we have credible security systems at CREEP and the RNC.

Wong spoke highly of him. So, he was interviewed, and he struck me as being an intense type, but had all the right answers regarding the Republican Party, the Nixon Presidency, etc. (He also had an eye for my Secretary. But so did most guys that met her. I guess there is something about those sexy French women.)

On that score (no pun intended!), an author wrote a bestselling Watergate book that focused negatively on McCord's role in Watergate, alleging he was inept and mysterious regarding his Watergate antics on the night of the break-in. The book included his famous placing of tape over the stairwell doors of the Watergate complex and inferred he was reporting back to the CIA about all that was going on. Pretty industrious, the reporter also found that McCord had rented an alleged "hideaway apartment" not too far from his residence. I'm sure it was for a legitimate business purpose.

McCord indicated to me that he had his own security company in Maryland and former CIA associates were participants. I shook his hand

and told him all looked good, but I would have to clear it with Ehrlichman, which I did. So, the deed was done and the rest is history; it was early January 1972—six months prior to Watergate.

Shortly after I left the White House staff to work as the Assistant Director, Enforcement, Alcohol Tobacco and Firearms in the spring of 1972, he called me and unbelievably made a "Corleone" offer I couldn't refuse, but sure did!

He said, "We have a new Latin team (subsequently part of the group to be infamously known as the Watergate burglars) and we are available for off-the-books electronic penetrations that your organization might need." I looked at the phone, not believing what I had just heard and said to myself, "For crying out loud, he's out there moonlighting wiretaps." I ended the conversation quickly, without direct comment on his offer. I tactfully lied and said I was on my way to an important meeting.

Where I went to school, you could go to jail just for talking like that on the phone. It's called conspiracy! McCord made me very nervous that day. I tried to dismiss the thought that I might well have erred in his hiring.

Enter, Chuck Colson, the hard driving, intelligent, efficient, political "nut cutter" extraordinaire (there I go again, Ronnie!). Within months of his White House arrival, he earned the title "wild man." One day, the always colorful Lyn Nofziger, now regrettably deceased, told me he was going to go over to see Haldeman about Colson's conduct and that it represented a White House hazard. He returned with a chagrined look and said, "Bob said, yeah, but he gets the job done."(*Oy Vey* or *Se La Vi*, here, take your pick!)

The Watergate time clock began to tick.

Keeping up with the salient players, enter one E. Howard Hunt—America's answer to James Bond. Former CIA, he actually had a distinguished career in the overthrow of the Arbenz regime in Guatemala in 1954. His dashing luck ran out, though, when he headed up the Bay of Pigs fiasco, under his *nom de guerre* "Edwardo."

Colson, a classmate of his at upscale Brown University in Massachusetts, was the fatal Watergate connection.

Immediately prior to his hiring, I got a call from Dean, who said the senior staff, then at a working session at the Western White House in San Clemente, wanted to bug an upcoming conversation in the White House between Hunt and a former CIA operative. I found out later that that operative was the famous Lucien Coneen, head of the CIA in Vietnam. Hunt supposedly wanted him to forge (in concert with Hunt) State Department embassy cables that would then show that JFK ordered the assassination of Diem, the President of Vietnam. (James Bond, I knew you were related to Howard!)

It was 3:00 p.m.; Dean said he wanted it done, forthwith. I said, "John, for crying out loud!" I then called a very unhappy Al Wong and told him to hurry up, put it in the office of lowly staffer John Brown. Dean called and said no; put it in the office of a higher up. (I was getting my Irish way up!)

Wong's guys put the cables in higher up Ken Coles' office, but then Dean called and said no, put it in Ehrlichman's office. Dean called and said Colson says that Hunt said, "The interviewee is on his way!"

By this time, it was 4:00 p.m. I said, "Holy Shit!"

Wong said, "No time for a bug, we put a recording machine under Ehrlichman's office couch."

I said, "*Bueno!*"

Hunt said, "Lucien, so good to see you, have a seat on the couch!" Coneen sat down, instantly killing the recording. An hour later, I then play the very first White House tape for Dean, whose eyes narrow, like a pissed off Lucky Luciano.

I finally said, "There ain't no more, John!" And with attempted tact, I indicated he was an asshole for letting that farce go forward. (I wonder why our relationship went downhill from there?)

Hunts' second White House assignment, was to sick his Latin team on Daniel Ellsberg, whose purloined Pentagon Papers were sent along to the New York *Times*, always willing to get a piece-of-cake, anti-Nixon scoop.

Hunt brilliantly decided that Ellsburg's psychiatrist had the skinny on the guy. (Who knows, maybe Hunt thought he could be driven crazy! Nah, Howard wouldn't do that.) The Latin team broke into the office with former prosecutor Gordon Liddy in the lead, taking pictures to prove (to whom? God knows) they were there. Ehrlichman signed off on the caper with a lawyerly caveat amounting to, "Don't get caught." He did eighteen months for that one sentence, courtesy of John Wesley Dean.

But ol' J. Edgar Hoover was delighted when the judge, Matthew Byrne, alerted by justice guys, summarily threw the hot potato out. (He certainly didn't know that the very straight judge was offered the FBI job by Ehrlichman. Good try, John!) Ellsberg's wife's maiden name was Marx, whose father was a close friend of Hoover.

I have often said the death of J. Edgar thirty days before the Watergate break-in, ensured that that powerful hand would not bail out Richard Nixon. He had the skinny on most of the Congressional membership and wasn't afraid to use that power to stay in power, for fifty or more years.

If you like conspiracy theories about his death, you'll like the one that says the ubiquitous Latin team did him in, via cyanide in his dessert (whew!), and whisked him away in a dark blue Volkswagen. (Of course!)

I met Hoover once in an elevator. I had always pictured him short, like the bulldog he was. I was surprised that he was about six foot. My buddy, Myles Ambrose, Commissioner of Customs at the time, tells a great story about him. He was in his office, talking with him, when Hoover suddenly hit a button under his desk, summoning his black valet. Myles thought it was coffee time. But no, all Hoover wanted was to have the valet close the window blinds. He executed that order flawlessly and silently with an almost imperceptible tilt of his head to the right.

I was called to testify before the Senate Watergate Committee in May of 1973. It was a most trying experience, which was fully covered by television and the world's media. I, frankly, did not know if my testimony would result in federal incarceration. I accepted that possibility, but was determined to make clear that I knew of no involvement of the President in the inane clemency message that John Dean dreamed up, and asked me to transmit to James McCord, the leader of the Watergate burglary team.

As indicated, John Ehrlichman publicly called Dean's actions in that regard, "a monumental error." Dean in his otherwise comprehensively detailed book, *Blind Ambition*, about his actions in the Watergate matter, failed to even mention this critical event in the Watergate drama.

My reaction to that critical exclusion today, is: "What goes around, comes around, John."

* * *

TUESDAY, MAY 22, 1973
U.S. SENATE, SELECT COMMITTEE ON PRESIDENTIAL CAMPAIGN ACTIVITIES
Washington, D.C.

Mr. Dash. Call Mr. John J. Caulfield, please.

Senator Ervin. Mr. Caulfield, stand up, please.

Hold up your right hand.

Do you swear that the evidence that you give the Senate Select Committee on Presidential Campaign Activities to be the truth, the whole truth and nothing but the truth, so help you God?

Mr. Caulfield. I do.

Senator Ervin. Mr. Caulfield, as I understand it, you will be available to the committee later if it wants to get you or to get any information from you other than that which you may give on this occasion?

Mr. Caulfield. I understand, sir.

Senator Ervin. Thank you.

Senator Baker. Mr. Chairman—

Senator Talmadge. Mr. Chairman, there is a vote going on.

Senator Baker. Before we proceed, I note that signal lights indicate that there is a roll call vote in progress in the Senate.

Might I suggest, Mr. Chairman, if the members of the committee agree, in the interest of time and expediency, that we might consider part of the committee going to vote now and part of it going at the 5-minute warning buzzer and permit this witness to begin, at least with the reading of his statement?

Senator Ervin. I think that would be very wise.

Mr. Dash. Mr. Caulfield, would you for the record, please state your full name and address?

TESTIMONY OF JOHN J. CAULFIELD, ACCOMPANIED BY JOHN P. SEARS, COUNSEL

Mr. Caulfield. My name is John J. Caulfield; I reside at 5208 Concordia Street, Fairfax, Va.

Mr. Dash. Are you accompanied at this hearing by an attorney?

Mr. Caulfield. Yes, I am.

Mr. Dash. Will the attorney please identify himself for the record?

Mr. Sears. My name is John P. Sears. I am an attorney in Washington, D.C.

Mr. Dash. Mr. Sears, there is another microphone.

Mr. Caulfield, you have a statement which you wish to either submit to the committee or read to the committee?

Mr. Caulfield. I would prefer to read it, Mr. Dash.

Mr. Dash. Every member of the committee, I understand, has received a copy of that. Would you now commence to read your statement?

Mr. Caulfield. Yes, sir; I will.

My name is John J. Caulfield. I was born on March 12, 1929, in the Bronx. N.Y. I was educated at the local parochial elementary school and Rice High School in Manhattan. Upon completion of my high school education I received a partial scholarship for basketball at Wake Forest University.

After 2 years I was forced to leave college owing to the fact that my family could not supply enough additional funds for me to continue my education. For a short time thereafter I worked as a bank teller before joining the New York Telephone Co. in 1949 as a draftsman.

In November of 1950 I was drafted into the U.S. Army where I served in the Signal Corps until I was honorably discharged in November of

1952. Prior to being drafted, I had taken the civil service examination for appointment to the New York City Police Department.

While still in the Army, I received notification that I had passed the examination and on June 1, 1953, I joined the police department as a patrolman. In August of that year, having graduated from the Police Academy, I was assigned to a Bronx precinct where I walked a beat and was assigned to a sector car which covered one area of the precinct.

Owing to an award which I received for the arrest and conviction of a ring of seven people involved in a series of robberies, I was promoted to the position of detective on September 25, 1955. Between that time and June of 1966, I was assigned to the Bureau of Special Services where my duties consisted of monitoring the activities of terrorist organizations and frequent assignment to VIP protective duties.

My activities in regard to militant terrorist groups consisted of monitoring and compiling intelligence on their overt activities, newspaper research, interviewing informants, investigating what relationships existed between these groups, and generally familiarizing myself with the progress of their activities. Examples of the groups which I investigated included the Communist Party, Cuban militant organizations, as well as a variety of Latin domestic revolutionary groups who planned or were suspected of planning various kinds of unlawful activities. During this time I received a number of awards in connection with my work, some of which were:

1. In 1958, I received a Meritorious Police Award owing to the seizure of a store of contraband weapons destined for Ireland. I might add parenthetically that my father has not yet gotten over that.
2. In 1959, I received an Excellent Police Award for arrest and conviction, in cooperation with the FBI, of the prime Castro agent operating in the United States in 1958.
3. In December 1964, I received a Meritorious Police Award for the arrest of the perpetrators of the bazooka shelling of the United Nations.
4. In 1965, I received an award for participating in the arrest and conviction of a group of French-Canadians and domestic militants who had plotted to destroy the Washington Monument, The Statue of Liberty, and the Liberty Bell.

My protective duties in regard to VIP assignments consisted, among other things, of coordinating the activities of the Secret Service agenda with the New York City Police Department in the political campaign of 1960. During the 1960 campaign I was assigned to both candidates when they visited New York and I got to know Mr. John Sherwood who was in charge at that time of Vice President Nixon's Secret Service detail.

Senator Baker. Mr. Witness, would you suspend for just a moment. The signal system indicates there is now 5 minutes before the end of the roll call.

Might I ask the committee if there is any objection to the witness continuing to read this statement in the presence of counsel, even though Senator Weicker and I as the only two committee members remaining have to go out now and vote. If there is any objection on behalf of the committee or on behalf of the witness or his attorney we will have to suspend. But inasmuch as your statement is 26 pages long and each member has a copy of it, if you have no objection, I suggest that we proceed.

Mr. Sears. We have no objection.

Mr. Caulfield. May I proceed?

Mr. Dash. Yes sir, proceed on behalf of the committee.

Mr. Caulfield. In May of 1968, I received a letter from Mr. Sherwood indicating that there was a possible position in the upcoming Nixon campaign for the Presidency for a person to serve in the security area. I telephoned Mr. Sherwood and substantiated what he had said in the letter and he told me that Mr. H. R. Haldeman would interview me if I were interested. Mr. Sherwood arranged an appointment for me with Mr. Haldeman at 450 Park Avenue in New York, which was the campaign headquarters, and I was hired.

With the assassination of Robert Kennedy in early June, my duties changed and ultimately, starting with the end of the 1968 convention, I became responsible to Mr. John Ehrlichman for being sure that the staff quarters and working areas of the Nixon campaign traveling staff were secure as we moved from city to city during the campaign. Mr. Ehrlichman was pleased with my work during this time, and on election night in 1968 he told me that in view of my work he would be happy to recommend me if I had any interest in obtaining a position with the Federal Government in Washington.

A few days after the election I called Mr. Ehrlichman in Key Biscayne, Fla., and told him I wished to be considered for the position of Chief U.S. Marshal. He told me that he would speak to Mr. Haldeman about this and get back to me. Subsequently a meeting was arranged with Mr. John Mitchell at the Pierre Hotel in New York which Mr. Mitchell told me that while my work was highly thought of, there had been a decision made to "semimilitarize" the U.S. Marshal's Office and therefore they were considering a retiring, high, military official for this post. Between December 1968 and April of 1959, I was interviewed for and pursued a variety of possible appointive jobs in Washington.

In late March 1969, I received a telephone call from Mr. Ehrlichman who asked me if I would visit him in his office a day or two later. I did so and at that meeting he asked if I would be willing to set up a private security entity in Washington D.C., for purposes of providing investigative support for the White House. I told him that I would think this over but by the time I had returned home that evening, I had decided that I did not wish to do this. I called him the next day with a counterproposal, namely, that I join the White House staff under Mr. Ehrlichman and, besides providing liaison functions with various law enforcement agencies, thereby be available to process any investigative requests from the White House. I mentioned to him that if he agreed with my proposal I would intend to use the services of one Mr. Anthony Ulasewicz who was a detective with the New York City Police Department nearing retirement. He said he would think about it and get back to me.

A few days later I received a call from his office asking if I would come to Washington to discuss the matter and that meeting resulted in my appointment to the White House staff on April 8, 1969.

My duties at that time consisted of being a White House Liaison with a variety of law enforcement agencies in the Federal Government, through arrangements worked out with Mr. Ehrlichman, Mr. Herbert Kalmbach, and Anthony Ulasewicz. Mr. Ulasewicz retired from the New York City Police Department and was paid on a monthly basis by the Kalmbach law firm, that employment commencing on July 9, 1969. During the next 3 years, first on orders from Mr. Ehrlichman and later in some instances, on orders from Mr. John Dean, Mr. Ulasewicz, under my supervision, performed a variety of investigative functions, reporting the results of his findings to the White House through me. I do not fully recall all of the investigations performed in this fashion but have available a list of those which I do recall if the committee wishes to examine it.

In July of 1970 Mr. John Dean became counsel to the President and Mr. Ehrlichman was named to the position of Presidential Assistant for Domestic Affairs. Thereafter I worked directly for Mr. Dean, but on occasion, Mr. Ehrlichman continued to call upon me directly for investigative work involving the services of Mr. Ulasewicz.

In the spring of 1971, I began to notice that, for some reason, the amount of investigation work handled by Mr. Ulasewicz through me had diminished. Much of the talk around the White House was becoming to center more and more on the 1972 Presidential election and I began to examine ways in my mind in which I might become involved. Since I had performed security duties in the 1968 election campaign, and realizing some of the security demands of a Presidential campaign, I wished to become involved in the security area of the campaign.

Toward that end, I composed a memorandum suggesting that an inside security capability be formed to handle the demand of the 1972 campaign. Such an organization would have a capability to perform various security functions to insure the security of the traveling staff, the Committee to Re-Elect the President headquarters, the convention site and would employ various guards and security people. In short, I was suggesting the formation of a capability to cover all the security needs of a Presidential campaign. The name I gave this suggested operation was "Sandwedge."

I further suggested that I leave the White House staff and set up this security entity, if it were approved, and suggested a budget of approximately $300,000 to $400,000. I gave the memorandum to Mr. Dean and got the strong impression from him that it went to higher levels, but I have no knowledge of who saw it. During the summer of 1971, I inquired of Mr. Dean as to the state of my proposal on numerous occasions but ultimately was told by Mr. Dean that he didn't think my suggestion was "going anywhere."

I was disappointed that my memorandum had been refused. I next spoke with Mr. Dean concerning obtaining a position as a personal aide to John Mitchell, when he became campaign director. Mr. Dean agreed to ask

Mr. Mitchell if such a position was available; he did so and on November 24, 1971, he accompanied me to an interview at Mr. Mitchell's office.

I explained to Mr. Mitchell that what I wanted was a position similar to that occupied by Dwight Chapin in relation to the President and that in addition to handling the kinds of activities that Chapin handled for the President; I could be of value to Mr. Mitchell as a bodyguard. Mr. Mitchell listened to what I had to say but was noncommittal as to what status I would occupy with him. He said, however, that we would "get that all straightened out when I arrived at the reelection committee." He was unsure as to when he would join the reelection committee but thought that it would be sometime in January or February of 1972. I left his office and walked back to the White House by myself. Mr. Dean remained and as I was walking through Mr. Mitchell's outer office I noted Mr. Gordon Liddy sitting with Mr. Dean evidently waiting to see Mr. Mitchell.

At that time, I was sure I had a position with Mr. Mitchell but the nature of my duties was quite unsettled. Ultimately, on the 1st of March 1972, I went to the reelection committee to commence my duties there. It soon became clear to me that Mr. Mitchell regarded me only as a bodyguard which was not what I had in mind at all. During March I took two trips with Mr. Mitchell outside of Washington, one brief trip to New York City and the other to Key Biscayne, Fla. Since Mr. Mitchell regarded me as his personal bodyguard I carried a revolver in my briefcase.

By the time the trip to Florida occurred in late March, I was already in touch with a friend of mine at the Treasury Department about possible employment there. After being in Florida for approximately 2 to 3 days, I received word that my house in Fairfax, Va., had been burglarized and so I flew home to attend to my wife and family. Mr. Fred LaRue had joined us in Florida after our arrival and upon my departure, he asked that I leave my revolver in his possession since Mr. Mitchell would "feel better" if there were a revolver on the premises. I gave my revolver to him and ultimately received it back in May of 1972, after LaRue had given it to Mr. James McCord for safekeeping upon Mr. LaRue's return from Florida.

Once I returned from Florida I performed no more duties of any kind for Mr. Mitchell and had formally decided to seek employment at the Treasury Department which I ultimately obtained. In April, I started working for the Treasury Department and then became staff Assistant to the Assistant Secretary of Treasury for Enforcement and on July 1, 1972, I became Acting Assistant Director for enforcement, Bureau of Alcohol, Tobacco, and Firearms.

In September of 1971, I received a call from Mr. Barry Mountain of the Republican National Committee who informed me that John Ragan was leaving his duties as security officer for the national committee, the Republican National Committee.

He asked me if I knew of anyone who would be interested in the position and I said no, but that I would check around. I subsequently asked Mr. Al Wong, a Deputy Assistant Director of the Secret Service, if he knew of anyone to recommend for such a position. He told me that he could recommend highly a former colleague and retired CIA agent, Mr. James McCord, and gave me his telephone number. I then called Mr. McCord and invited him to my office for an interview with him; I called Mr. Mountain and arranged for Mr. McCord to see Mr. Mountain. He did so, and was thereafter hired by the Republican National Committee.

Since before leaving his employment, Mr. Ragan had intended to handle security for the Committee To Re-Elect the President offices as well as the national committee, it was natural that Mr. McCord upon being hired by the national committee was soon interviewed by Mr. Robert Odle, the office manager of the Committee To Re-Elect the President and in late December or early January Mr. McCord was hired by the Committee To Re-Elect the President also. I had been consulted about him by the reelection committee and recommended him for this position also.

Between our original meeting in September of 1971, and June of 1972, Mr. McCord and I grew to be personal friends even though we did not physically see each other frequently with the exception of the month of March 1972, when I saw him on a daily basis at the Committee to Re-Elect the President. During this period we casually discussed on some occasions the possibility of going into business together after the election campaign was over and Mr. McCord felt quite beholden to me since he felt that I had been responsible for his employment at the national committee and the Committee to Re-Elect the President.

In May of 1972, we had lunch together at the Hay Adams Hotel in Washington. I had just begun my assignments at the Treasury Department and we discussed my plans and hopes for expanding my duties and he stated at that time that I should "keep him in mind" if I was looking for consultant help in carrying on investigations.

In July of 1972, and that date may well be wrong and I don't know as my recollection of the date was July of 1972, in July of 1972 after his arrest, I had Mr. Ulasewicz call his home and tell him to go to a designated public telephone booth near his house where I would be calling him. I called him at that public telephone and simply asked him if there was anything I could do for him or his family at this time of personal difficulty. No one had asked me to make this call and I was motivated entirely by my own personal concern for his condition and that of his family.

To deviate a bit here I noticed Mr. McCord indicated here his conversation with me on that occasion coming of a story relative to a double agent Alfred Baldwin. I do recall him mentioning that, I did not when I made this statement that is in fact correct.

Dear Jack --- I am sorry to have to tell you this but the White House is bent on having the CIA take the blame for the Watergate. If they continue to pursue this course, every tree in the forest will fall and it will be a scorched earth. Jack, even you will be hurt in the fallout.

I examined the letter and found that it was postmarked in Rockville Md., and thereby believed that the letter was from James McCord because he lived in Rockville. I called Mr. Dean's office and spoke with Mr. Fielding, an assistant to Mr. Dean, and read the letter over the telephone to him. Thereafter I went to Mr. Dean's office and gave him the letter.

In early January of 1973, I was attending a drug conference in San Clemente, Calif. when I received a telephone call in my hotel room from Mr. John Dean. He asked that I go outside the hotel and call him back from a public telephone, which I did. He told me that he had a very important message which he wanted me to deliver to James McCord, that Mr. McCord was expecting to hear from me and McCord would understand what the message referred to. He said the message consisted of three things:

1. "A year is a long time;"
2. "your wife and family will be taken care of;"
3. "You will be rehabilitated with employment when this is all over."

I immediately realized that I was being asked to do a very dangerous thing and I said to Mr. Dean that I did not think it was wise to send me

89

on such a mission since Mr. McCord knew, as many others did that I had worked closely with Mr. Dean and Mr. Ehrlichman at the White House and therefore it might be quickly guessed that any messages I was conveying were probably from one of the two. The reason I raised this question with him was because, very frankly, I did not wish to convey the message. Mr. Dean asked if I could think of any other way to do it and I suggested that perhaps I could get Mr. Ulasewicz to convey the message over the telephone anonymously stating that the message had come from me.

Mr. Dean felt this would be all right so I hung up the telephone and called Mr. Ulasewicz in New York. He did not wish to convey the message at first but I convinced him to do it merely as a matter of friendship to me. Mr. Ulasewicz call Mr. McCord's home, and presumably, delivered the same message which Mr. Dean had given to me. He then called me back in California, and reported that he had delivered the message and that Mr. McCord's attitude had been one of satisfaction. I was glad to hear this since I had felt this probably meant that Mr. McCord had been in some stage of negotiation about his status and that this message had probably relieved his mind.

At this point in time, my impression was that obviously there had been some negotiations going on between Mr. Dean's office and Mr. McCord in regard to Executive clemency, such negotiations probably being carried on through third parties and that Mr. McCord had wanted to hear the message which was transmitted to him through a reliable source, such as myself.

I called Mr. Dean and told him that the message had been delivered by Mr. Ulasewicz and that Mr. McCord had seemed satisfied.

The next day I received another telephone call from Mr. Dean at my hotel in which he said that Mr. McCord wanted to see me as soon as I got back. I objected to seeing Mr. McCord, but finally Mr. Dean got my concurrence to do so. My impression was that Mr. McCord wanted to say something to me and I was not instructed to say anything more that what had been in the message to him.

I called Mr. Ulasewicz and asked him to arrange a meeting with Mr. McCord the following evening when I was to arrive back in Washington. Mr. Ulasewicz called me back and said Mr. McCord had agreed to meet with me at the second overlook on the George Washington Parkway but that, different from Mr. Ulasewicz's last conversation with Mr. McCord, Mr. McCord sounded quite irritated and annoyed.

Owing to a delay in my airplane flight from California I was unable to meet with Mr. McCord on the night of January 11 as I had intended. When I arrived in Washington on the evening of January 11, I did attempt to call Mr. McCord but was told by a member of his family that he had retired for the evening. Mr. Ulasewicz had already conveyed instructions to Mr. McCord for holding our meeting on Friday night, January 12. At approximately 7 that evening I met with Mr. McCord at the second overlook on the George Washington Parkway. He joined me in my car and as I recall the conversation, I first apologized to him for my delay in getting to see him due to my presence in California and the late arrival of my airplane. I also said I was sorry if he had been irritated by receiving the anonymous calls from my friend.

He said something like, "OK, that's OK Jack." I said, "I guess you received the message then?"

Mr. McCord then said words to the effect: Jack, I am different from all the others. Anybody who knew me at the CIA knows that I always follow my own independent course. I have always followed the rule that if one goes [I took this to mean going to jail] all who are involved must go. People who I am sure are involved are sitting outside with their families. I saw a picture in the newspaper of some guy who I am sure was involved sitting with his family. I can take care of my family. I don't need any jobs, I want my freedom.

I stated that I was only delivering the message and had nothing to do with its formulation or had no control over what was being done. I sympathized with Mr. McCord's situation and made remarks such as, I can't understand how this all happened, I'd give anything if I had not recommended you for your two jobs with the Republican Party.

I did try to impress upon Mr. McCord that I was simply a messenger and was not too pleased to even be doing that. I did say that the people who had asked me to convey the message had always been honorable toward me and that I thought it was a sincere offer.

He asked me who I was speaking with at the White House and I said I could not reveal any names but that they were from the "highest level of the White House."

He continually said that all he was interested in was his freedom and that he was not pleased that others who he felt had been involved were not suffering the consequences that he was. In the context of demanding his immediate freedom, he said that he know of a way in which his freedom could be obtained and asked me if I could convey his plan to the people at the White House with whom I was talking.

His plan, simply, was as follows: On two occasions, one in September 1972 and the other in October 1972, Mr. McCord told me that he had called telephone numbers at foreign embassies in Washington and he stated he was sure these embassies were subjects of national security wiretaps. On both occasions he had stated that he was a man involved in the Watergate scandal and, without giving his name, had inquired as to the possibility of acquiring visas and other traveling papers necessary to travel to these foreign countries.

It was Mr. McCord's theory that if the Government searched its wiretap records, it would find records of these two calls. Meanwhile Mr. McCord and his attorneys would make motion in court, aimed at dismissing the case against Mr. McCord because of the use of wiretap evidence by the prosecution. Mr. McCord's idea was that when the U.S. attorney was told that at least two of Mr. McCord's conversations had been intercepted over a national security wiretap he would be forced to dismiss the case rather than reveal that the two embassies in question were the subject of national security wiretaps.

Mr. McCord was quite adamant in saying that he was sure the Government could secure his immediate release if they wanted to help him and, other than the publicity incumbent on the Government for being forced to dismiss the case against him, such an approach would save the administration any real embarrassment. He gave me a note with the dates of the two conversations that he referred to and told me that he knew this kind of thing had been done before, most recently in the *Ellsberg* case and that he saw no reason why the Government could not at least accomplish this for him. I told Mr. McCord that I would get back to him on the wiretap situation and would probably be calling him in a day or two to set this up. I agreed to carry this message concerning wiretaps back to the White House and the meeting ended.

At no time in our first meeting do I recall saying anything about the President but I specifically renewed the offer of Executive clemency as indicated above and referred to it as coming from "the highest levels of the White House." At some point in the conversation Mr. McCord said to me, "Jack, I didn't ask to see you." This puzzled me since my clear understanding from Mr. Dean was that McCord had specifically asked to see me.

In any event, I called Mr. Dean on Friday night, January 12, and reported that Mr. McCord did not seem interested in accepting the offer made in Mr. Dean's original message to him, that Mr. McCord wanted his immediate freedom and that he, Mr. McCord, felt that he had a way to obtain that freedom. I then mentioned over the telephone, McCord's idea for securing his freedom because of the use of national security wiretaps and said that I wished to discuss this matter directly with Dean.

The following day I saw Mr. Dean in his office in the White House and explained to him Mr. McCord's suggestion for obtaining his freedom, as Mr. McCord had described to me. Mr. Dean said, "Well, I'll check on that." He then turned the conversation back to the offer of Executive clemency. To the best of my knowledge he said, "Jack, I want you to go back to him – McCord – and tell him that we are checking on those wiretaps but this time impress upon him as fully as you can that this offer of Executive clemency is a sincere offer which comes from the very highest levels of the White House."

I said, "I have not used anybody's name with him, do you want me to?"

He said, "No, I don't want you to do that but tell him that this message comes from the very highest levels."

I said, "Do you want me to tell him it comes from the President?"

He said words to the effect, "No, don't do that; say that it comes from way up at the top."

I told Mr. Dean I would get back to Mr. McCord and that indeed; I had told Mr. McCord that I would.

At the meeting with Mr. Dean he also impressed upon me that this was a very grave situation which might someday threaten the President that it had the potential of becoming a national scandal and that many people in the White House were quite concerned over it. Mr. Dean said that none of the other then-defendants in the Watergate burglary "were any problem," and that Mr. McCord "was not cooperating with his attorney."

I have been asked at the U.S. attorney's office and by Senate investigators, and have tried as best I can to recall what impressions I had at this particular point in time. As best as these impressions I can be stated, I believed that I was going back to see Mr. McCord to again extend an offer of Executive clemency and that by my doing so I was doing a great service for the President of the United States in a very sensitive matter. At no time, either before or after this meeting with Mr. Dean did I ever speak to any other White House officials about this offer of Executive clemency. I specifically never spoke to the President of the United States and have no knowledge of my own as whether he personally had endorsed this offer or whether anyone had ever discussed it with him. Since I had worked extensively for Mr. Dean and Mr. Ehrlichman had formed an impression that Mr. Dean rarely made decisions on matters of consequence without speaking to Mr. Ehrlichman, my guess was that when Mr. Dean referred to "high White House officials" he at least meant Mr. Ehrlichman. I know that he was in conversation with someone about my contacts with Mr. McCord since, when I was in his office on January 12, he received a telephone call and I heard him say, "I'm receiving a report on that right now" to the party on the other end.

At any rate, I then called Mr. McCord and arranged a meeting with him again at the second overlook of the George Washington Parkway early in the afternoon on Sunday, January 14. On this occasion we both got out of our cars and walked down a path from the overlook toward the Potomac River.

This meeting lasted only 10 to 15 minutes. I did most of the talking. I told Mr. McCord that the White House was checking into the wiretapping situation and that I had been asked to impress upon him once again that the offer of Executive clemency was a sincere and believable offer coming from the very highest levels of the White House. I explained to him that among the reasons why I believed that such a commitment would be kept were that the White House officials with whom I was in contact were extremely concerned about the Watergate burglary developing into a major scandal affecting the President and therefore such a promise would not be given lightly. I told him that the White House officials with whom I was talking were complaining because they felt that Mr. McCord was the only one of the Watergate burglary defendants who was refusing to cooperate. At no time on this occasion or on any other occasion do I recall telling Mr. McCord to keep silent if called before the grand jury or any congressional committees.

Senator Ervin. Mr. Caulfield, we have another vote. I think maybe you had better pause until we get back.

[Recess]

Senator Ervin. The committee will resume.

Mr. Dash. Mr. Caulfield, you were in the midst of your statement I suggest you go back a sentence or two so we will have continuity.

Mr. Caulfield. I will pick up a couple of sentences, Mr. Dash.

I told him that the White House officials with whom I was talking were complaining because they felt that Mr. McCord was the only one of the Watergate burglary defendants who was refusing to cooperate. At no time on this occasion or on any other occasion do I recall telling Mr. McCord to keep silent if called before the grand jury or any congressional committees.

His response to my conversation was that he still wanted his immediate freedom and he felt strongly that if the White House had any interest in helping him secure that freedom that they could do something about the two telephone calls which he was sure had been intercepted. I told him I would check on this matter again and get back to him.

I was not attempting exert pressure on Mr. McCord by telling him of comments I was hearing from the White House; merely, I was attempting to let him know the kinds of things I was hearing from Mr. Dean concerning the White House's attitude toward him if that would be of assistance to him.

Later on Sunday I telephoned Mr. Dean to report on my meeting with Mr. McCord. I told him that in my opinion Mr. McCord has absolutely no interest in the offer of Executive clemency. I told Mr. Dean that Mr. McCord was still adamant in his belief that the White House had the power to have the charges against him dismissed if it would merely pursue the wiretaps which he had mentioned. Mr. Dean said that I should tell him that there wasn't much likelihood that anything would be done about the wiretap situation and, in response to my comments about McCord's refusal to consider Executive clemency he said something like, "Well, what the hell does he know anyway?"

Mr. Dean told me to go back to Mr. McCord again and "commiserate" with him but he did not ask me to renew the offer of Executive clemency. I guessed that the reason why he wanted me to see Mr. McCord again was simply to maintain a friendly relationship with him in case there was a need for any further conversation with him through me. I probably would have met again with Mr. McCord anyway, since I felt badly about his predicament and I considered him a good friend. In any event, on Monday, January 15, I called Mr. McCord to report that nothing seemed to be happening in regard to the wiretap situation. He became quite angry over the telephone and reaffirmed his belief that if the White House really wanted to help him they could do so by using the method he had suggested and that he knew that Mr. Magruder (who was then going to be a Government witness) was going to perjure himself. I also mentioned getting together with him but he said he had no interest in seeing me unless I had something more to talk to him about. He was quite upset so I did not pursue the matter further.

On Tuesday, January 16, I again called him in an attempt to meet with him and he again was highly irritated about the White House's failure to do something about the wiretap situation and again mentioned Mr. Magruder. I said I would inquire further about the wiretaps and I might have something for him "in a week or so."

Subsequently I called him and arranged to meet with him again, the exact date of this meeting being unsure in my mind. We again met at the overlook on the George Washington Parkway, he got into my car and we drove out the parkway, pursuing a course in the general direction of Warrenton, Va. I have no specific recollection as to how long we drove but I would say that it was an hour or two.

I would characterize this conversation as a very friendly one in which a large portion of the time was spent discussing our respective families, how my job at the Treasury Department was going, and various other purely personal matters. I gave him my private telephone number at the Treasury Department and told him that if he or his wife ever wanted me to do anything for them, they should feel free to call me, to simply use the name "Watson" and I would know who it was. Frankly, this was merely a device to save me from any possible embarrassment.

I do not have a specific recollection as to how it arose, but I believe he asked me if he was still the only one of the Watergate defendants that the White House was concerned about. I said that I thought he was, but that I had no knowledge of what relationship existed between the White House and the other Watergate defendants. He said that the Cuban were quite nervous and in his opinion, might make a statement at any time and that I "could pass that along for whatever it was worth."

I told him there was absolutely no hope, in my opinion, of the White House ever doing anything about the wiretap situation and asked him when he thought he might make a statement. He said that he had not decided that yet, but that he had spoken to his wife and family and that he felt free to make a statement whenever he thought the time was right.

I again asked if there was anything I could do for him. He said one thing that I could do was to see whether bail money could be raised for him pending an appeal in his case. I said I would check into this.

Toward the end of our conversation, realizing that he definitely was going to make a statement on the Watergate burglary at a time of his choosing and that such a statement would in all probability involve allegations against people in the White House and other high administration officials, I gave him what I considered to be a small piece of friendly advice.

I said words to the effect that, "Jim, I have worked with these people and I know them to be as tough-minded as you and I. When you make your statement don't underestimate them. If I were in your shoes, I would probably do the same thing."

I later called Mr. Dean and advised him of Mr. McCord's request for bail funding and he said words to the effect that, "Maybe we can handle that through Alch." Sometime later, Mr. Dean called me and asked me to tell McCord that the bail money presented too many problems and that maybe consideration could be given to paying premiums. I later called McCord and reported this. His reaction was "I am negotiating with a new attorney and maybe he can get it handled." This is the last conversation I had to date with James McCord.

Although this is a lengthy statement, I wish to make two further points: At no time in any conversations with Mr. McCord did I advise, pressure, or threaten him in an attempt to make him accept the offer of Executive clemency. I viewed my role simply as one of a messenger and while I tried to give both Mr. Dean and Mr. McCord the full flavor of what was going on at both ends of this message-transacting process, I actively refrained from injecting myself into the process at either end. I realized at the time of my first conversation in January that I was involved in questionable activity but I felt that it was important to me to carry this message for the good of the President.

I have previously testified before the grand jury and have spoken on two other occasions with the U.S. attorney's office and have spoken on two occasions as well with Senate investigators. Although I have discussed the matter of whether any of my actions could be viewed as violations of the criminal law with my attorney and have been advised of the availability and privileges and possible attempts of securing immunity from prosecution, at no time have I refused to answer any questions in regard to my conduct and I have felt that it is more important that I be able to speak freely about my involvement in actions herein, than to have whatever protection might be rightfully mine under my constitutional and executive privileges. I hope that what I have to say here today will assist the committee in its investigations and if, upon hearing of all the facts, it is thought that I am guilty of some wrongdoing I will still feel that the truth is my best defense.

Senator Baker. Mr. Caulfield, we thank you very much for your lengthy but very useful statement. It is now 4:10 in the afternoon. The chairman has been called to the floor of the Senate to participate in the debate on a matter now pending on which we will shortly vote. Before he left the committee he suggested that we conclude your prepared statement today on the condition that you and your attorney are agreeable to returning in the morning at 10 o'clock so that the committee and staff can proceed with interrogation. Is that satisfactory to you?

Mr. Caulfield. Absolutely, Senator.

Senator Baker. Then, the committee will stand in recess until 10 o'clock tomorrow morning.

[Whereupon, at 4:10 p.m., the hearing was recessed, to reconvene at 10 a.m., Wednesday, May 23, 1973.]

WEDNESDAY, MAY 23, 1973
U.S. SENATE, SELECT COMMITTEE ON PRESIDENTIAL CAMPAIGN ACTIVITIES
Washington, D.C.

The Select Committee met, pursuant to recess, at 10 a.m., in room 318, Russell Senate Office Building, Senator Sam J. Ervin, Jr. (chairman), presiding.

Present: Senators Ervin, Talmadge, Inouye, Montoya, Baker, Gurney, and Weicker.

Also present: Samuel Dash, chief counsel; Fred D. Thompson, minority counsel; Rufus L. Edmisten, deputy chief counsel; Arthur S. Miller, chief consultant; Jed Johnson, consultant; David M. Dorsen, James Hamilton, and Terry F. Lenzner, assistant chief counsels; Barry Schochet, assistant majority counsel; Donald G. Sanders, E. William Shure, and Robert Silverstein, assistant minority counsels; Joan C. Cole, secretary to the minority; Pauline O. Dement, research assistant; Eiler Ravnholt, office of Senator Inouye; Robert Baca, office of Senator Montoya; Ron McMahan, assistant to Senator Baker; A. Searle Field, assistant to Senator Weicker; Mare Lackritz, Ron Rotunda, assistant counsels; Eugene Boyce, hearings counsel; John Walz, publications clerk.

Senator Ervin. The committee will come to order. I would like to reiterate what I stated yesterday that Mr. Caulfield is to return later and that the questions at this appearance will be restricted to matters dealing with the communications between him and Mr. McCord. In respect to the questions of counsel ------

Senator Gurney. Mr. Chairman, May I inquire what the plan of the committee is on the witness following Mr. Caulfield?

Mr. Dash. Yes, the witness following Mr. Caulfield will be Tony Ulasewicz who will be the individual who has been identified as the person who made the telephone call to Mr. McCord and that he will be called specifically to testify as to that role. He too will be available, Senator Gurney, to come back and to testify on other matters which he has to testify before this committee.

Senator Gurney. Mr. Chairman, as I understand that last evening counsel interviewed the attorney, the former attorney, for Mr. McCord and that his statements were in startling conflict and contrast with what

Mr. McCord had told us here the other day and I would think it would be extremely important that we get this witness on just as soon as possible and I, as one committee member, would like to see him on this afternoon and I think his testimony is in total conflict with what Mr. McCord said and I think he should be called just as soon as we can get him just before the recess before we call Tony.

Mr. Dash. We can do that, Mr. Chairman. It is true Mr. Alch did come in and did request he be called and we thought we would call him immediately after Tony Ulasewicz but there is no reason why he could not be called immediately after Mr. Caulfield.

Senator Gurney. I wish he might.

Senator Baker. Mr. Chairman, let me make a suggestion, if I may, I think Senator Gurney's point is well taken. However, in the interest of continuity and in keeping with the preparation of the committee let me make an alternative suggestion, if I may. Let us finish with Mr. Caulfield today, Mr. Chairman, I would suggest, which I think we can do in a reasonably short period of time since Mr. Caulfield, I understand, is agreeable to return and to explore other matters, unrelated directly with the subject matter of his testimony thus far that we go forward then with the next witness who is----

Mr. Dash. Tony Ulasewicz, which I think will only take about 10 minutes.

Senator Baker. After we finish that we will call Mr. Alch and that will result in some continuity and the also be in accord with Mr. Gurney's request. I am sure Mr. Alch will be on the stand today.

Senator Gurney. That is what I want to be sure, he does get the stand. We have taken a good deal of time in the questioning in fact, I have used my own fair share but I do think it is awfully important that we get Mr. Alch on today because his testimony is going to be in such sharp contrast and contradiction to what we learned from Mr. McCord earlier and I think we ought to get it to clear up some of these things that are hanging around the room here.

Senator Weicker. Mr. Chairman, it is my understanding then that only so we might present a logical picture we will restrict our questions to the matters that Mr. Caulfield raised yesterday in his testimony but certainly that there are no restrictions and no cause as to future testimony and that he will be recalled for any questions we want to ask, is that correct?

Senate Ervin. That is correct.

Senator Weicker. Thank you very much.

Mr. Dash. Mr. Caulfield, because your statement was a lengthy one, and there was a recess over the evening, let me seek to briefly summarize the essential highlights of your statement that you gave to the committee, and please correct me if anything I say is not consistent with your understanding of your statement.

In December of 1972 you received an unsigned note which you understood came from Mr. McCord which complained of a White House effort to blame CIA for the Watergate and threatened that "all the trees in the forest will fall," if this effort continued.

In early January 1972, while you were in California, you received a telephone call from John Dean from Washington asking you to deliver the following message to Mr. Dean.

"1. One year is a long time. 2. Your wife and family will be taken care of. 3. You will be rehabilitated with employment when this is over."

You did not want to deliver the message but you thought that it could be delivered through Mr. Tony Ulasewicz and Mr. Dean agreed to do it that way.

Mr. Caulfield. Mr. Dash, can I interrupt a second, the correct pronunciation is Ulasewicz.

Mr. Dash. Ulasewicz.

Mr. Caulfield. Right.

Mr. Dash. You did call Mr. Ulasewicz and you asked him to deliver this message, and although he himself at first was reluctant he did agree to deliver the message and he did call Mr. McCord and reported back to you that Mr. McCord appeared satisfied and you reported this to Mr. Dean.

The following day you received another call from Mr. Dean informing you that Mr. McCord wanted to see you when you returned to Washington. You had Ulasewicz arrange the meeting which was set for Friday, January 12, at the second overlook on the George Washington Parkway. In substance you emphasized that you were only a messenger, that the offer you were conveying of Executive clemency was from the highest levels of the White House, and that it was a sincere offer. Mr. McCord's response in substance was that he wanted his complete freedom and even suggested a plan which involved proffering that the Government had wiretapped his telephone calls that he had made two to foreign embassies whose phones he believed were wiretapped. You do not recall saying anything about the President to Mr. McCord but you did transmit an offer of Executive clemency to Mr. McCord which you told him came from the highest levels of the White House. You reported this meeting to Mr. Dean on the telephone. The following day you met with Mr. Dean and he told you to go back to Mr. McCord and impress upon him as fully as you could that the offer of Executive clemency was a sincere offer and when you asked if you should mention any names, such as the President, he said no, but told you that you should say that the offer came "from way up top." Mr. Dean also expressed his concern over this matter as a grave situation that could threaten the President and could become a national scandal. That none of the other defendants in the Watergate case were any problem and Mr. McCord was not cooperating with his attorney.

You again met with Mr. McCord at the second overlook on the George Washington Parkway on January 14 for a short while, and conveyed the message of concern over a national scandal which could threaten the President and that Mr. McCord was the only one of the defendants not cooperating. Again, McCord expressed his interest to you in securing his freedom and wanted you to do something about the wiretaps he had mentioned to you earlier.

You telephoned Mr. Dean that same day and told him that Mr. McCord was not interested in Executive clemency, and that Mr. McCord believed that the White House could help him get the charges dismissed by supplying proof of the wiretaps for him.

You had a final meeting with Mr. McCord on a date you cannot recall but about the third week in January where you picked him up in your automobile on the second overlook on the George Washington Parkway and drove for about an hour or 2. At this time you told him that the White House could not do anything for him about the wiretap problem and there was a lengthy conversation which for the most part involved other subjects than Watergate. You concluded during that conversation that Mr. McCord definitely was going to make a statement on the Watergate burglary and it would probably involve allegations against people in the White House and other high administration officials. You gave him what you indicated to the committee as friendly advice to the effect, "Jim, I have worked with these people and I know them to be tough-minded as you and I. When you make your statement don't underestimate them. If I were in your shoes I would probably be doing the same thing."

You also had received from Mr. McCord some reference of request to do something about bail and you were not able to accomplish anything on the bail issue during further contacts with him. That in no time did you talk with the President about this matter or mention the President to Mr. McCord concerning the offer of Executive clemency but that you carried this message to Mr. McCord because you felt it was for the good of the President.

Is that basically a fair summary of the gist of the contacts with Mr. McCord and Mr. Dean that were contained in your statement?

Mr. Caulfield. Yes, sir.

Mr. Dash. Now, although you state that you made no mention of the President to Mr. McCord during the meeting, you do know, or you do not, that the President is the only person in this country who can grant Executive clemency in a Federal criminal matter?

Mr. Caulfield. Yes, sir I do.

Mr. Dash. Did you understand when you were speaking with Mr. Dean that Mr. Dean wanted you to transmit the message to Mr. McCord that the offer of Executive clemency was made with the proper authority?

Mr. Caulfield. Yes, sir.

Mr. Dash. Was it your intention during the meetings with Mr. McCord to leave him with the clear understanding that the person with authority to make such a representation of Executive clemency were in fact extending this offer to him?

Mr. Caulfield. Just repeat that for me, Mr. Dash?

Mr. Dash. Yes.

Was it your intention during your meetings with Mr. McCord to leave him with the clear understanding that persons with authority to make such a representation as to the Executive clemency were in fact extending this offer to him?

Mr. Caulfield. Yes, sir.

But, of course, I have not and did not at that time have any direct knowledge that the President had made such an offer, endorsed such an offer, or in any way was involved in that offer.

Mr. Dash. I understand that.

Mr. Caulfield. Right.

Mr. Dash. Looking back, Mr. Caulfield, what do you see your role to have been in this relationship and what did you think about it?

Mr. Caulfield. Well, as I have indicated in my statement, Mr. Dash, I viewed myself as a messenger between Mr. Dean and Mr. McCord, exchanging information back and forth on the ongoing negotiations, which obviously had been taking place prior to the time that I had received the telephone call in California.

Mr. Dash. And was it your understanding at that time, especially with the discussions you had with Mr. Dean, that there was serious concern at the White House, at least Mr. Dean was conveying to you, involving a possible scandal, that there was a real effort to get Mr. McCord to accept this offer because of the concern or trouble that he might be able to raise in the Watergate case?

Mr. Caulfield. That was my clear impression, Mr. Dash, yes sir.

Mr. Dash. And you were being asked to do this because of your friendly relationship with Mr. McCord?

Mr. Caulfield. That is correct.

Mr. Dash. I have no further questions, Mr. Chairman.

Senator Ervin. Mr. Thompson?

Mr. Thompson. Thank you.

Mr. Caulfield, as I understand it, you have been a personal friend of Mr. McCord's, is that correct?

Mr. Caulfield. That is correct, sir.

Mr. Thompson. Would you still say that relationship exists as far as you are concerned?

Mr. Caulfield. Yes, sir, I still consider Jim McCord my friend.

Mr. Thompson. As you were talking to him about the possibility of Executive clemency and he was responding to you, what would you say, according to what he told you, his primary interest was?

Mr. Caulfield. Very frankly, sir, as I reflect back upon the conversation, it is very clear in my mind that Jim McCord was concerned about his freedom and was taking the steps that he believed to gain that freedom totally. He was uninterested in any deals of a year is a long time or other statements like that. He, in that first conversation at the car, made it crystal clear to me that he was different from the others, that I could check it if I wanted to, that he wanted his freedom, period.

Mr. Thompson. In other words, he was not necessarily disinterested in any deals, but he was not interested in any deals that would not produce his freedom. Is that a correct statement?

Mr. Caulfield. That is correct. That is correct.

Mr. Thompson. As you state here in your statement, he continually said that all he was interested in was his freedom and he was not pleased that some of the others that had been involved were not suffering as he was suffering, is that correct?

Mr. Caulfield. That is correct.

Mr. Thompson. You referred also in your statement to his plan, a plan which he had which he thought would produce his freedom. I believe you referred to his two telephone calls in September and October of 1972 to two embassies.

Mr. Caulfield. Yes sir.

Mr. Thompson. According to what he told you, was it your impression that he believed that these two calls were made in order to ultimately produce his freedom, put the Government in an embarrassing position, and therefore produced his freedom?

Mr. Caulfield. Yes sir.

Mr. Thompson. All right, now. Let me ask you about your relationship with Mr. Ehrlichman for just a few moments.

How long did you work for Mr. Ehrlichman when he was counsel for the President?

Mr. Caulfield. From the day that I arrived at the White House on April 8, 1969, formally, through July 1970, when Mr. Ehrlichman moved over to the Domestic Council, and then on an informal basis from that time until the time I worked at the White House.

Mr. Thompson. Then after Mr. Ehrlichman left the Office of Counsel for the President, Mr. Dean was his successor; is that correct?

Mr. Caulfield. Yes sir.

Mr. Thompson. You remained, then, under Mr. Dean; is that correct?

Mr. Caulfield. That is right.

Mr. Thompson. Did you have any contact or any continuing relationship with Mr. Ehrlichman after Mr. Ehrlichman left to go to the Office of Domestic Affairs?

Mr. Caulfield. Well, only on rare peripheral matters relative to the investigations that I indicated in my statement.

Mr. Thompson. And while you were working for Mr. Ehrlichman directly, as I understand it, you had possibly more than one function with one of those to carry out certain investigations?

Mr. Caulfield. Yes, I had many other functions, sir but that was one small part of my duties at the White House.

Mr. Thompson. And you continued to do some of this matter for him pursuant to his direction after you left that office?

Mr. Caulfield. On very rare occasions, sir.

Mr. Thompson. Would you on some occasions act as an intermediary between Mr. Ehrlichman and Tony Ulasewicz, for jobs which Mr. Ulasewicz would do?

Mr. Caulfield. Yes sir.

Mr. Thompson. Would you say that would be on frequent occasions?

Mr. Caulfield. That would be infrequent after July of 1970.

Mr. Thompson. But occasionally.

Mr. Caulfield. Oh, yes; yes sir.

Mr. Thompson. Now, Mr. Caulfield, in your statement here, you state that you were guessing that Mr. Dean probably was referring to Mr. Ehrlichman when he referred to high White House sources?

Mr. Caulfield. Yes, that was my guess.

Mr. Thompson. That was your guess at that time?

Mr. Caulfield. Yes sir.

Mr. Thompson. You also state, "I know he was in conversation with someone about my contact with Mr. McCord, because when I was in his office on January 13, he received a telephone call and I heard him say 'I am receiving a report on that right now'."

Were you referring to Mr. Ehrlichman?

Mr. Caulfield. No; what I am saying is that the call came in, that there were no names mentioned. Mr. Dean said, I am receiving --- there was, apparently the party calling made some comments. Mr. Dean said "I am getting a report on that right now."

Mr. Thompson. Oh, I see, this conversation that you overheard was Mr. Dean with someone?

Mr. Caulfield. I mean in Mr. Dean's presence, Mr. Counsel.

Mr. Thompson. I see. And you assumed that that conversation perhaps was with Mr. Ehrlichman or possibly with Mr. Ehrlichman.

Mr. Caulfield. Possibly with Mr. Ehrlichman, but I have no way of knowing sir.

Mr. Thompson. You feel very definitely in your mind that he was talking with someone else about it, is that correct?

Mr. Caulfield. I want to be careful there, sir, because I just do not know where the call came from. If it was coming from within the White House, then it was someone in the White House. So – by that I mean, sir, there is an interoffice telephone system. Now, I do not know and have no way of knowing whether that was an interoffice call or whether or not it was a call coming from outside. So that is why I mentioned it that way.

Mr. Thompson. What would you say was the relationship between Mr. Dean and Mr. Ehrlichman during this period of time? Did Mr. Dean in many matters in effect report to Mr. Ehrlichman?

Mr. Caulfield. Yes, sir.

Mr. Thompson. Or answer to Mr. Ehrlichman?

Mr. Caulfield. Yes sir; on many matters having to do with Mr. Dean's work as well.

Mr. Thompson. Did you ever talk with Mr. Ehrlichman about this matter, this business of possible Executive clemency for Mr. McCord with anyone?

Mr. Caulfield. No, sir.

Mr. Thompson. Did you ever talk to anyone there at the White House besides Mr. Dean?

Mr. Caulfield. Absolutely no one but Mr. John Dean.

Mr. Thompson. I have no further questions, Mr. Chairman.

Senator Ervin. If there is no objection, I would like to exchange places for questioning witnesses with Senator Montoya and let him take my place and I will take his place.

Senator Montoya. Thank you, Mr. Chairman.

Senator Ervin. There are no objections. You may proceed.

Senator Montoya. Thank you, Mr. Chairman.

Mr. Caulfield, I think we had better get your background and employment duties at the White House in better perspective. What exactly were you doing when you went to work at the White House in April of 1969?

Mr. Caulfield. My prime duties at the White House were to act as liaison primarily with the U.S. Secret Service and other Federal law enforcement agencies. As I indicated, I worked under Mr. Ehrlichman; Mr. Krogh was under Mr. Ehrlichman as well. From time to time, I would be assigned major projects that came up in the law enforcement area.

For example, shortly after coming to the White House, I was assigned to the then-emerging drug abuse task force that subsequently emerged as Operation Intercept.

Senator Montoya. Well, were you working directly under Mr. Ehrlichman? Or were you working under Mr. Dean?

Mr. Caulfield. No, Mr. Dean, sir was not at the White House at that time. This is – you asked – I think the question was what my duties were when I went into the White House? When I went into the White House, Mr. John Dean was not yet there. He was at the Justice Department.

Senator Montoya. As I understand, you went to work at the White House in April 1969 and you worked there until March 1972.

Is that correct?

Mr. Caulfield. Yes, sir.

Senator Montoya. All right.

Were you on the payroll of the White House or were you being paid by someone else?

Mr. Caulfield. No, sir.

Senator Montoya. And were you assigned to the White House payroll or were you on the Treasury payroll?

Mr. Caulfield. I don't quite understand.

Senator Montoya. Were your working or being paid from the payroll attributable to the Department of the Treasury or to the White House?

Mr. Caulfield. The White House payroll, sir.

Senator Montoya. All right.

Mr. Caulfield. Yes, sir.

Senator Montoya. Now, did you come in contact quite frequently with Mr. Ehrlichman?

Mr. Caulfield. In the course of my duties, yes, sir, not on a daily basis certainly but I would be working with his staff people Mr. Egil Krogh when I first went in there, as I have indicated I would be assigned major projects. I was the White House representative for the Marihuana and Dangerous Drugs Task Force that began in the spring of 1969.

Senator Montoya. All right.

Mr. Caulfield. Well, Mr. John Ehrlichman, when I was working for him coming aboard the White House was counsel to the President. When Mr. Ehrlichman became the Presidential assistant and headed up the Domestic Affairs Council, Mr. John Dean came in and became the counsel to the President, and I remained in the office of the Counsel to the President under Mr. Dean, my direct supervisor.

Senator Montoya. Did he assign many things to you?

Mr. Caulfield. Yes, sir.

Senator Montoya. Did Mr. Ehrlichman continue to assign things to you to do?

Mr. Caulfield. As I have indicated, Senator, only on rare occasions after Mr. Ehrlichman became Assistant to the President for Domestic Affairs.

Senator Montoya. Did Mr. Haldeman assign things to you?

Mr. Caulfield. On only one or two occasions that I could recall Senator. Very rarely, in fact almost never.

Senator Montoya. All right.

You mentioned that you had interviewed Mr. McCord for his employment at the executive offices and recommended him to go to work for the Committee to Re-Elect the President. That is correct isn't it?

Mr. Caulfield. Well, that is essentially correct sir. The recommendation was for employment at the Republican National Committee initially and flowing from that Mr. McCord was hired by the Committee to Re-Elect.

Senator Montoya. How many interviews did you say you had with Mr. McCord?

Mr. Caulfield. I recall two. I recall a luncheon when it was already established that he was on board.

Senator Montoya. Who did you clear with at the White House before he recommended Mr. McCord for that appointment?

Mr. Caulfield. I didn't clear anybody, sir.

Senator Montoya. Who did you call at the Republican National Committee?

Mr. Caulfield. I called Mr. Barry Mountain who was the then deputy chairman for administration.

Senator Montoya. Had he asked you to recommend someone?

Mr. Caulfield. Yes, sir.

Senator Montoya. Was there a job classification for the individual that he wanted?

Mr. Caulfield. No, as I recall, the way Mr. Mountain explained it to me they wanted someone to come up and do a security survey and possibly following the survey the part who did the survey would be hired as a supervisor of security at the Republican National Committee.

Senator Montoya. Was there any discussion with respect to that classification that the man who would be chosen and the man that you might interview should be qualified in espionage activities for the party?

Mr. Caulfield. Absolutely not, sir.

Senator Montoya. Were you aware that that was one of the competencies that this man should have anyway?

Mr. Caulfield. No, sir.

In reviewing Mr. McCord's qualifications they appeared to me from career experience in security work to be absolutely outstanding, and his credentials appeared to be impeccable.

Senator Montoya. What did you conceive with respect to the game plan that was going on at the time?

Mr. Caulfield. I beg your pardon?

Senator Montoya. Mr. McCord mentioned that you had told him that he was ruining the game plan. What did you conceive that to be?

Mr. Caulfield. Well, sir, I do not recall Mr. McCord saying "game plan" but it was obvious to me that there were negotiations going on with respect to this Executive clemency for Mr. McCord.

Senator Montoya. Then let me read to you from Mr. McCord's statement on page 9. I read as follows: "I refused to discuss it. He stated that I was fouling up the game plan. I made a few comments about the game plan." That was Mr. McCord's statement on page 9. Do you recall that conversation?

Mr. Caulfield. I do not recall those words, Senator.

Senator Montoya. Well, what words akin to that were uttered by you in the presence of Mr. McCord?

Mr. Caulfield [conferring with counsel]. Senator I am a little confused on your asking me – I have no recollection of Mr. McCord – of me saying to Mr. McCord he was fouling up the game plan. My statement does not indicate that.

Senator Montoya. Well, let me read an extended text of the statement. On page 9 "About 10 o'clock a.m., on Thursday, January 25, 1973, in a meeting lasting until about 12:30 a.m. we drove in my car toward Warrenton, Va., and returned, and a conversation ensued which repeated the offers of Executive clemency and financial support while in prison and rehabilitation later. I refused to discuss it. He stated that I was fouling up the game plan. I made a few comments about the game plan."

Mr. Caulfield. Yes, sir.

Mr. Montoya. You recall that?

Mr. Caulfield. No, sir, I do not. As I indicated in my statement this trip here was one of friendly conversation between two friends. I have no recollection of offering him Executive clemency on this occasion. I have no recollection about stating that I was fouling up the game plan.

Senator Montoya. Did Mr. Dean tell you why he was calling you to get in touch with Mr. McCord?

Mr. Caulfield. When was that?

Senator Montoya. When he called you at San Clemente.

Mr. Caulfield. He indicated to me that he had a very important message that he wanted to be delivered to James McCord.

Senator Montoya. I understand that. But did he tell you why he had chosen you for that mission?

Mr. Caulfield. No, sir, he did not.

Senator Montoya. Did you ask him?

Mr. Caulfield. No, sir. He knew, of course, that I had known Jim McCord.

Senator Montoya. How did he know? Had you discussed Jim McCord with him?

Mr. Caulfield. I had been over to the committee. Eventually after he was hired I am sure I mentioned to Mr. Dean that the fellow McCord is hired, he appears to be outstanding. He was well aware that I knew Jim McCord; there were no questions in anybody's mind.

Senator Montoya. Did you get in touch after Watergate with Mr. Dean to indicate to him about your friendship with Jim McCord?

Mr. Caulfield. Would you repeat that, Senator, please?

Senator Montoya. Did you get in touch with Mr. Dean and communicate your friendship with Jim McCord?

Mr. Caulfield. When, sir?

Senator Montoya. After the Watergate break-in.

Mr. Caulfield. We had conversation. I expressed shock on many occasions that James McCord was arrested at the Watergate.

Senator Montoya. No, but the point I am trying to make, Mr. Caulfield, is that you had two or three interviews with Mr. McCord they were short in duration.

Mr. Caulfield. Yes, sir.

Senator Montoya. Preliminary to his being hired?

Mr. Caulfield. Yes, sir.

Senator Montoya. There were other people at the Republican National Committee and at the Committee to Re-Elect the President ---

Mr. Caulfield. Yes, sir.

Senator Montoya. [continuing] Who knew Mr. McCord better than you did, presumably because he worked with them for a longer time and I am wondering why Mr. Dean selected you to carry on this mission of offering Executive clemency to Mr. McCord when there were other people within the organization of the national committee and the CRP who had developed a better and more intimate acquaintance with Mr. McCord.

Mr. Caulfield. Well, of course, I am sure that Mr. Dean trusted me, and in reading some of the things that might have gone on before there was apparently a need for someone from the White House to bring a message to him, and certainly Mr. Dean knew that I knew Jim McCord, and then I would like to reiterate that I received a letter in December which I had brought to Mr. Dean's attention wherein it was alleged that the White House was involved in attempting to place the blame on CIA. So all of these things Mr. Dean knew. Mr. McCord sent me the letter; Mr. Dean knew that.

Senator Montoya. Did you ever inquire of Mr. Dean when he was telling you just what to say to Mr. McCord, did you ever inquire from him as to the high sources and who they were?

Mr. Caulfield. Well, sir, in the first telephone call this was all telling you just what to say to Mr. McCord. Subsequently, as I have indicated in my statement, we did have a conversation after the first meeting.

Senator Montoya. Now, you mentioned that Mr. Dean had instructed you to say that it comes from way up at the top.

Mr. Caulfield. Yes, sir.

Senator Montoya. What did you conceive that to be at the time?

Mr. Caulfield. Well, sir, in my mind I believed that he was talking about the President. Although, again ------

Senator Montoya. How would you have interpreted that without any further explanation? The same way?

Mr. Caulfield. I do not understand, Senator.

Senator Montoya. You mentioned that it was your impression that it must have come from the President. Now, did you, when you reached that impression, question Mr. Dean any further about it?

Mr. Caulfield. No, sir.

Senator Montoya. My time has run out so I will not pursue that any further.

Thank you, Mr. Chairman.

Senator Ervin. Senator Gurney.

Senator Baker?

Senator Baker. Mr. Chairman, I would like to follow your example. I would offer to yield to Senator Weicker at this point. I believe that he may or may not wish to yield to Senator Gurney.

Senator Weicker. Mr. Chairman, I just have two or three brief questions; then I will yield.

Mr. Caulfield, turn to page 19 of your testimony. You state there, "I have been asked by the U.S. Attorney's Office and by Senate investigators and am trying as best I can to recall what impressions I had at this particular point in time. As best as these impressions can be stated, I believe that I was going back to see Mr. McCord to again extend an offer of Executive clemency and that by my doing so I was doing a great service for the President of the United States in a very sensitive matter."

My first question to you, very simply, is this: using your own words I would like you to comment and explain to me why it is – why it is – that you thought you were doing a great service for the President of the United State?

Mr. Caulfield. Well, sir, to go back a little bit, it was a great honor for me to serve as a member of the President's staff. I had come from a rather humble background, a police officer. I did receive this great opportunity to serve on the Presidents staff. I felt very strongly about the President, extremely strongly about the President. I was very loyal to his people that I worked for. I place a high value upon loyalty. Now, out of the blue, I am injected into this scandal, I am being asked by one of my former superiors to deliver a message that I know to be Executive clemency. I tried to avoid it, as my statement indicates. I imposed upon my friend to do it, hoping that all parties would be satisfied. I was not successful.

I was brought back in again to it, now being asked to see Mr. McCord directly. I did go to see him.

Now I am becoming further implicated into this matter. I had this conversation with John Dean, who was the counsel to the President. I had been there 3 years. I know what the relations are and how they exist. I make certain judgments based upon those relationships. In my mind, I felt that the President probably did know about it.

Now, I am going out the door, to become more specific, and it crossed my mind that this conceivably was for the President. I believed it. I had to think about that. And based upon all of that background, I believed I was doing something for the President of the United States, and I did it, sir.

Senator Weicker. Mr. Caulfield, you have lived a life dedicated to the law. In the very beginning of your statement, you cite a career, a very fine career, one that was recognized time and time again. Let me ask you this question.

I read on page 24 of your testimony, where you are talking to McCord and where you have given a friendly piece of advice, and you say, "Jim, I have worked with these people and I know them to be as tough-minded as you and I. When you make your statement, don't underestimate them. If I were in your shoes, I would probably do the same thing."

I read that, and you tell me if I am wrong, as the testimony of a man who is in conflict. On the one hand delivering a message to a friend; on the other hand, a man whose whole career has been dedicated to honesty and seeing the truth come out. Would that be a fair description of a conflict that was occurring within you at that time?

Mr. Caulfield. There was a definite conflict, Senator. You are absolutely right. I know when wrongdoing is occurring. I have indicated here that I knew that the offer of Executive clemency in this matter was wrong, yes sir, I knew that. But what I am saying to you sir, is that my loyalties, and especially to the President of the United States, overrided those considerations.

Senator Weicker. So actually, there was a conflict between your loyalties, and it is interesting that you used the very word that I had in a written question before you made your statement. Did you feel, at this moment in time, a conflict between your loyalties to the President and a life dedicated to law and to the pursuit of truth?

Mr. Caulfield. Yes, sir. That is correct. And also that I was hopefully being able to help a friend.

Senator Weicker. Then lastly, Mr. Caulfield, on page 25, you state: "That I realize that at the time of my first conversation in January that I was involved in questionable activity but I felt that it was important for me to carry this message for the good of the President." Was there a conflict in your mind between doing an act for the good of the President and an act that would be for the good of the country?

Mr. Caulfield. That is a tough question, Senator. All I can say is what I did what I did for the reasons I have stated.

Senator Weicker. I have no further questions.

Senator Ervin. Senator Talmadge?

Senator Talmadge. Mr. Chairman, at this time, I yield to the distinguished Senator from Hawaii, Mr. Inouye.

Senator Inouye. Thank you very much.

Mr. Caulfield, am I to conclude from your responses to Senator Weicker, that you were aware that you were involved in a criminal act of obstructing criminal investigations?

Mr. Caulfield. Yes, sir.

Senator Inouye. For a man on the Kalmbach payroll doing espionage work, to go through some very secretive process to get in touch with him makes me ask: Why all this secrecy when, as you have stated, it was just to convey your sympathies to Mr. McCord? Why did you go through all this secret movement? Were you afraid that the phones were tapped?

Mr. Caulfield. Are you speaking about my call to, asking Mr. Ulasewicz to call James McCord, sir?

Senator Inouye. Yes, why did you go through all that secret stuff to get in touch with Mr. McCord. According to your statement, all you wanted to say is I feel sorry for you, can I do anything for you. Is that right?

Mr. Caulfield. Yes, sir. To have spent a career in security work as I have, and as Mr. McCord had, and to watch the daily accounts of the Watergate developments from June 17 on, it certainly occurred to me, sir, that any conversations taking place over Mr. McCord's home telephone conceivably could have been the subject of some type of wiretapping by either governmental parties or other people who were concerned about Mr. McCord. Plus the fact, sir – well, I should go back a little bit.

That impression, and Mr. McCord, I understand, has indicated that he had the same concerns, indicated to me that a circuitous route, if I wanted to speak to him, would be the appropriate way to do it, sir.

Senator Inouye. I would like to call your attention to page 16 of your prepared remarks, in which you describe Mr. McCord's plan. This plan called for Mr. McCord's calling two foreign embassies and telling the official in such embassies that he was a defendant in the Watergate case and requesting a visa. From this, did you gather that Mr. McCord was trying to blackmail the U.S. Government?

Mr. Caulfield. No, sir.

Senator Inouye. Or were you aware that if he carried out this plan it would place in jeopardy the national security of the United States of America?

Mr. Caulfield. That is a two part question, now.

Are you asking did I think this was a blackmail?

Senator Inouye. Yes.

Mr. Caulfield. No sir; I didn't think that this was a blackmail, I viewed this as an attempt on the part of a man who was distraught, who wanted his freedom and had come across a means of obtaining that freedom. I did not consider it to be blackmail, sir. I considered it, base upon my conversation with Mr. McCord, that he was distraught.

Senator Inouye. Didn't you think that there was a risk of compromising the security apparatus of the United States? As he pointed out, the Government would have to dismiss the case or admit that there were taps on these two embassies.

Mr. Caulfield. Well, sir, again in passing these messages back and forth, and I passed this one back to Mr. Dean, certainly a matter of this type would, in my judgment, work its way up to any question of policy and national security.

Senator Inouye. Did you think that this was a reasonable plan?

Mr. Caulfield. I thought it was an interesting one, sir.

Senator Inouye. You didn't think it was illegal or dangerous?

Mr. Caulfield. Sir, again, it is possible that these thoughts crossed my mind, but I have no recollection of it. And again, I am being put in a position of being a messenger and I was focusing on that. I wasn't giving consideration to all of the nuances, serious nuances that would be included.

Senator Inouye. Now as you sit here as a witness, do you consider that that plan was dangerous or illegal?

Mr. Caulfield. I can't judge that, Senator. It is certainly a serious matter.

Senator Inouye. Do you think it is proper to set up a government in a trial like this?

Mr. Caulfield. No, I don't think it is proper to set up the government, sir.

Senator Inouye. On page 24, this is one sentence that puzzles me. It says, "When you make your statement, don't underestimate them."

What did you mean by that?

Mr. Caulfield. Well, as I indicated in the statement, this was an extremely friendly conversation, Senator, I don't know if this has come through in my statement. We were talking now for an hour, an hour and a half about families, my boys, his children, his wife, my job. He gave me the suggestion that he might be able to help me in liaison with the Post Office, as I recall. This was all a very cordial conversation under very difficult conditions amongst friends.

Now, as I indicated I was convinced in my mind that he was going to go ahead at some point in time and make a statement. And looking at the broad picture, I could envision an ordeal for him, significant ordeal. He could be effectively on the other side of the people that I was talking to.

I was a friend. I don't know if he fully appreciated that, but that was the intent of my remarks, to let him know.

Senator Inouye. You were giving him friendly advice?

Mr. Caulfield. That is right, sir.

Senator Inouye. You were giving him friendly advice?

Mr. Caulfield. Yes, sir. That is right, sir.

Senator Inouye. Not to underestimate it, what did you mean?

Mr. Caulfield. Not to underestimate the tough-mindedness of all the players in this game.

Senator Inouye. What did you think that the other side would do to Mr. McCord?

Mr. Caulfield. I had no idea. It is apparent that Mr. McCord apparently has misinterpreted that, looking at his statement but that was not the intention. I would say that to a friend that was about to make a major decision that would be tough and I did.

Senator Inouye. I thank you very much, Mr. Chairman.

Senator Ervin. Senator Gurney.

Senator Gurney. Thank you, Mr. Chairman.

Mr. Caulfield, your testimony certainly has been very full and very clear. I just want to press home one or two points.

Referring to the previous testimony by Mr. McCord, at page 320 of the record, he had this to say about his conversations and meeting with you.

"Caulfield stated that he was carrying the message of Executive clemency to me from the very highest levels of the White House. He stated that the President of the United States was in Key Biscayne, Fla., that weekend," referring to the weekend following January 8, following meetings that we were in then, and that the President had been told of the results of the meeting."

Did you ever learn that the President had learned of the results of any of your meetings with Mr. McCord?

Mr. Caulfield. Absolutely not, sir.

Senator Gurney. He also stated this further on in the testimony on the next page. "Mr. McCord. He," meaning you, "further stated 'I may have a message to you at our next meeting from the President.'"

Did you ever tell him that?

Mr. Caulfield. No, sir.

Senator Gurney. Did you ever have any communication with the President of the United States with regard to this so-called Executive clemency offer to Mr. McCord?

Mr. Caulfield. None whatsoever, sir.

Senator Gurney. Did you ever hear Mr. Dean in any of you conversations with Mr. Dean ever refer to the fact that he had informed the President of any of these messages?

Mr. Caulfield. No, sir.

Senator Gurney. Did Mr. Dean ever say to you, "The President has instructed me to make this offer of Executive clemency to McCord through you," or through anybody else as far as that is concerned?

Mr. Caulfield. Absolutely not, sir.

Senator Gurney. Did you ever apply any pressure to Mr. McCord in any of these meetings for him to do anything in regard to the upcoming trial?

Mr. Caulfield. No, sir.

Senator Gurney. Did you ever urge him or advise him to plead guilty?

Mr. Caulfield. Never.

Senator Gurney. This point has been covered but it is important because of Mr. McCord's testimony. My understanding is that your understanding about these calls to the Embassy and the wiretaps at the Embassies that this was his theory of defense, a way that he could get out of it by having the case dismissed if these wiretaps had occurred, is that correct?

Mr. Caulfield. That is correct.

Senator Gurney. Did Mr. McCord ever discuss with you what other plans he might have if he were found guilty at the trial?

Mr. Caulfield. No, sir.

Senator Gurney. One final question. You served for some time under Mr. Ehrlichman in the White House. For how long a period?

Mr. Caulfield. From April 8, 1969, through July of 1970.

Senator Gurney. Did you see quite a bit of him during this time?

Mr. Caulfield. No, sir; I would not characterize my time under Mr. Ehrlichman as frequent visits. I would be working very close with his staff people, primarily Bud Krogh, who had a variety of duties in the Federal law enforcement area, and I would work primarily through Mr. Krogh into Mr. Ehrlichman.

Senator Gurney. But you were generally familiar with some of the missions or the work that Mr. Ehrlichman was carrying on in the White House is that fair to say?

Mr. Caulfield. Generally familiar, yes, sir.

Senator Gurney. Would you say that it was also a fair thing and say that Mr. Ehrlichman undertook a great many missions, a good deal of work in the White House, in his duties on his own, on his own independent carrying out, is that a fair thing to say?

Mr. Caulfield. Well, of course, I have no way of knowing Senator.

Senator Gurney. Would that be your impression?

Mr. Caulfield. It is possible, Senator,

Senator Gurney. I do not have any further questions, Mr. Chairman.

Senator Ervin. Senator Talmadge.

Senator Talmadge. Mr. Caulfield, are you still on the Federal payroll?

Mr. Caulfield. I am in what they call administrative leave state because of these developments with the Treasury; yes, sir of this moment, yes, sir, I am still on the Federal payroll.

Senator Talmadge. Getting a check?

Mr. Caulfield. Yes, sir.

Senator Talmadge. But you are on leave?

Mr. Caulfield. Yes, sir.

Senator Talmadge. Did you call Mr. John Ehrlichman immediately after the break-in at the Watergate on June 17?

Mr. Caulfield. Yes, sir.

Senator Talmadge. What did he say?

Mr. Caulfield. Well, I received a telephone call on the afternoon of June 17, which is the date of the break-in, the date of the break-in about 3 or 4 p.m., as I recall, from a gentleman I worked with in the U. S. Secret Service, Mr. Patrick Boggs, and he called me and he said, "Do you know Jim McCord?" and I said "Yes, I know Jim McCord." And he indicated, he said: "Well, we have received a report that there was a break-in at the Democratic Nation Committee. We are concerned because of our protective capabilities or responsibilities, rather, in that area. We have some agents checking into it. Some of the people appear not to have given their correct names and we are getting a report that one of those not giving the correct name is Jim McCord."

He said "Now, do you want to call John Ehrlichman or should I call him?"

After I had recovered from the shock, I indicated: "Well, you go ahead and try and reach him and I will try and reach him as well."

And I called the White House board and I was told that he was enroute to his residence. By the time that I did reach him Mr. Boggs had already contacted him. And I said to Mr. Ehrlichman, I said, "John, it sounds like there is a disaster of some type. Did you speak to Mr. Boggs?" He said, "Yes, what is this all about?" I said, "I haven't' got the foggiest notion what it is all about but they are saying they believed Jim McCord, who works for the committee, has been arrested in a burglary at the Democratic National Committee."

He said, I forgot what he said exactly, I think it was a long silence, as I recall, and I said, "My God, you know, I cannot believe it." He said, "Well, I guess I had better place a call to John Mitchell." I said. "I think that would be very appropriate." [Laughter.]

Senator Talmadge. Who said it sounds like a disaster, you or Mr. Ehrlichman?

Mr. Caulfield. John J. Caulfield.

Senator Talmadge. Why did you have Mr. Ulasewicz call Mr. McCord rather than calling McCord yourself?

Mr. Caulfield. In this July call?

Senator Talmadge. Yes. This anonymous, mysterious call with the New York accent. [Laughter.]

Mr. Caulfield. Are we talking about the January call or the July call?

Senator Talmadge. We are talking about the call with no name that Mr. Ulasewicz is alleged to have made at your request and the request of John Dean.

Mr. Caulfield. Oh, well again I did not want to make the call Senator. I knew how serious it was, how dangerous it was, I explained to John Dean that I did not want to do it. I had to focus completely on the seriousness of the misconduct but intuitively I know that I was wrong, and I just did not want to do it, and as I have indicated in my testimony I tried to get out of it and I felt that because I had asked Mr. Ulasewicz previously to set up this telephone arrangement with Mr. McCord outside of his residence that he could, when Mr. McCord received a call he would, understand that it was coming from me.

This was my way of getting the message delivered without getting involved.

Senator Talmadge. Whom were you working for at the time you relayed Mr. Dean's message to Mr. McCord?

Mr. Caulfield? In January?

Senator Talmadge. Yes, sir.

Mr. Caulfield. I was the Assistant Director of the Bureau of Alcohol, Tobacco and Firearms.

Senator Talmadge. Now, on behalf of whom did you assume Mr. Dean to be speaking, talking of when he spoke of Executive clemency to Mr. McCord?

Mr. Caulfield. Well, as I have indicated coming from Mr. Dean, having worked with him, I assumed that there were others at the White House who were involved in this matter in terms of the offer.

Senator Talmadge. Who did you think was the real author of the message, Mr. Dean or someone else?

Mr. Caulfield. Well, sir, again I believe conceivably, very conceivably, that if we are going to talk about others that quite possible Mr. Ehrlichman. I had no way of knowing that, Senator.

Senator Talmadge. Mr. Chairman, I have no further questions, thank you, sir.

Senator Ervin. Senator Baker?

Senator Baker. Mr. Chairman, thank you very much.

Mr. Caulfield I won't take very long but necessarily I expect the points I want further elaboration on in the questions I have may be at least in part repetitious. Do you have any idea why Mr. McCord chose you to send that letter to?

Mr. Caulfield. Well, I do not – of course, I do not know but Jim McCord knew I worked at the White House. He knew that I had worked for Mr. Dean.

Senator Baker. The answer is you don't know. Did Mr. McCord ever tell you why?

Mr. Caulfield. No, sir. He did not.

Senator Baker. Did he confirm that he wrote the unsigned letter to you?

Mr. Caulfield. Yes. I think there was just a brief conversation about it on our first conversation in the car.

Senator Baker. Did he indicate to you why he wrote the letter at all? You have told me now that he did not indicate why he chose you to write the letter – did he indicate to you why he wrote the letter?

Mr. Caulfield. I think in substance what he said was what was in the note, you know, the CIA, the White House will do this thing to the CIA, I am not going to stand for that.

Senator Baker. Did he tell you why the White House was going to blame this on the CIA?

Mr. Caulfield. No, sir, I have no recollection of that as to why.

Senator Baker. He didn't elaborate on that point at all?

Mr. Caulfield. No, sir.

Senator Baker. Did you have any indication or evidence or suspicion that the White House was trying to "blame it on the CIA" independent of your conversation with Mr. McCord?

Mr. Caulfield. Senator, the whole letter was – upset me quite a bit. You know it was unsigned and I assumed it was Mr. McCord, and the last sentence bothered me.

Senator Baker. Did you ask him why he felt they were going to blame it on the CIA?

Mr. Caulfield. No, sir.

Senator Baker. Mr. Caulfield, it seems to me that a defendant in those circumstances or a suspect who had been arrested on charges such as Mr. McCord had been arrested, have three possible alternative courses of action. I am speaking now in the hypothetical sense: He can plead guilty; he can plead not guilty and defend himself on the facts; or third, he can try to contrive a way to create circumstances which would result in his exoneration separate and apart from the rest.

Would that be the range of possibilities that presented themselves to Mr. McCord at the time?

Mr. Caulfield. In my judgment?

Senator Baker. Yes, sir.

Mr. Caulfield. Yes, sir.

Senator Baker. Now let's focus on the third. Obviously he pled not guilty. This record has reference, extensive reference, to efforts allegedly to induce him to plead guilty and receive Executive clemency which he declined to do. He pled not guilty. He was convicted. But before his trial and conviction or at least during the time of his trial and before his conviction this conversation with you, as I understand clearly in my mind in relation to the alternatives that were available to Mr. McCord, at the time of this conversations the trial was going on or at least he had not been convicted yet, is that correct?

Mr. Caulfield. That is my recollection, yes, sir.

Senator Baker. The trial was actually in progress, was it not?

Mr. Caulfield. I am not absolutely certain, I believe it was but dates are ---

Senator Baker. And Mr. McCord told you he was not going to plead guilty. He was not interested in Executive clemency, he was not interested in the year, that that was a long time, that he wanted out free and clear, is that the essence of it?

Mr. Caulfield. That is the essence of it, Senator.

Senator Baker. And that he wouldn't settle for anything less?

Mr. Caulfield. That is right.

Senator Baker. And that to achieve that end he had arranged and contrived to phone two foreign embassies whose telephones he knew or suspected to be tapped, presumably illegally or at least embarrassingly to the U.S. Government so that those calls could be subpoenaed by his attorneys and produced in court as evidence of illegal surveillance so that the prosecution against him would have to be thrown out or at least so that the Government would be so embarrassed by these alleged taps on foreign embassies that they would dare not prosecute him further, is that fair intendment of what Mr. McCord told you?

Mr. Caulfield. Yes, sir.

Senator Baker. Mr. McCord was holding hostage either the embarrassment of the U.S. Government with respect to wiretaps on foreign embassies or he was holding hostage the illegality of those taps on foreign embassies. Was that the thrust of his design for a defense at the time of that conversation?

Mr. Caulfield. That is my interpretations, sir, of his comments at that time.

Senator Baker. Thank you very much.

Senator Ervin. Now, the trial had begun at the time you had these meetings with McCord in January?

Mr. Caulfield. Yes.

Senator Ervin. And presumably, McCord knew something about the conversations which are occurring between the defendants and their lawyers did he not?

Mr. Caulfield. Presumably, Senator, yes, sir.

Senator Ervin. And had you not heard alleged statements in the press or heard statements over the TV to the effect that since certain men, Barker and McCord, had previously worked for the CIA, that there was some suspicion that the CIA was involved?

Mr. Caulfield. I think probably in the minds of many people at that time, that was the suspicion. I do not know whether or not I suspected that. But, yes, sir.

Senator Ervin. Now, McCord knew you were a lawyer for the President and also knew you were his friend, did he not?

Mr. Caulfield. Yes, sir.

Senator Ervin. So he wrote you a letter which was susceptible of the interpretations that he was giving you a warning that there was no validity to the claim that the CIA was responsible for Watergate?

Mr. Caulfield. Yes, sir.

Senator Ervin. And did you not entertain the opinion after receiving that letter that Mr. McCord probably wrote it believing that you would communicate its contents to Mr. Dean, at whose instances you had interviewed McCord?

Mr. Caulfield. Yes, sir; and I did just that.

Senator Ervin. And you did that?

Mr. Caulfield. Yes, sir.

Senator Ervin. Now, you testified under the questioning of Senator Weicker to the effect that your training in law enforcement had given you a conviction that it was wrong to attempt to suppress testimony by an offer of Executive clemency.

Mr. Caulfield. No question about that, Senator.

Senator Ervin. And also that you had a sense of loyalty to the President?

Mr. Caulfield. That is correct, Senator.

Senator Ervin. And also that you considered Jim McCord your friend and appreciated the fact that he was in a very unfortunate situation and you were motivated not only by your loyalty to what you thought, the loyalty to the President and by what assurance you had received from Mr. Dean that if McCord did not go along with the other defendants and cooperate with his lawyer, that there might be a scandal against the President?

Mr. Caulfield. That is exactly right, Senator.

Senator Ervin. So you were compelled to choose between your loyalties, and that was the reason you were willing to carry the message from Dean to McCord, notwithstanding the fact that you did not approve of offering Executive clemency in return for suppressing the testimony?

Mr. Caulfield. Yes, sir.

Senator Ervin. Well, it is proof of what my old philosophy professor told me, that the greatest trials we have in this world is when you are compelled to choose between different loyalties, some of which are conflicting. And you were trying to protect the President, you were trying to aid a friend, and you were trying to carry out a mission which you accepted somewhat reluctantly from the man that you knew – that is, John Dean – whom you knew to be the President's counsel and whom you knew would be actuated by the desire to protect the President against any scandal?

Mr. Caulfield. Absolutely correct, Senator.

Senator Ervin. Now, when you performed this mission for John Dean on these three occasions, what did you expect or, rather, what did you understand was expected of McCord in return for Executive clemency?

Mr. Caulfield. I believed that in terms of the context of the message, a year is a long time that it would be some time less than a year.

Senator Ervin. Did you infer from your conversation with Dean that under Dean's statements, McCord was expected to plead guilty, keep silent, receive a short sentence, and then receive clemency?

Mr. Caulfield. If he accepted the offer, that would be the way I would interpret it, yes, sir.

Senator Ervin. Now, you were asked a question if Mr. Ehrlichman did not do some things on his own accord, on his own authority.

For whom was Mr. Ehrlichman working?

Mr. Caulfield. Sir, he was working for the President of the United States.

Senator Ervin. Did you know of your own knowledge of any time that Mr. Ehrlichman did things on his own accord, out of his own head and imagination?

Mr. Caulfield. I am sure he has many time, Senator.

Senator Ervin. And are you unable to tell me whether he was acting on instructions or acting out of his own head and imagination?

Mr. Caulfield. No, sir. If I were given an assignment, I would go ahead and do it.

Senator Ervin. And when you called Mr. Ehrlichman shortly after the break-in, in June, or sometime in July, you think Mr. Ehrlichman told you he thought he had better call John Mitchell and you said you thought it would be a good idea?

Mr. Caulfield. Yes, sir.

Senator Ervin. That is all I have.

Senator Baker. Mr. Chairman, might I ask one more question?

Senator Ervin. Yes.

Senator Baker. Mr. Caulfield, you have testified at length and extensively about matters of great importance in which you had a direct involvement.

Mr. Caulfield. I beg your pardon, Senator.

Senator Baker. Mr. Caulfield, you have testified at length and extensively about important matters in which you had a direct involvement?

Mr. Caulfield. Yes, sir.

Senator Baker. You are aware of the nature of those transactions?

Mr. Caulfield. Yes, sir.

Senator Baker. And the possible consequences from them?

Mr. Caulfield. Yes, sir.

Senator Baker. Mr. Caulfield, have you ever been requested to or have you ever suggested that there be any claim of Executive privilege on your behalf?

Mr. Caulfield. No, sir.

Senator Baker. Have you ever requested immunity from prosecution from this committee, a grand jury, or anyone else with respect to the information you have given?

Mr. Caulfield. Absolutely not, sir.

Senator Baker. Thank you, sir.

Senator Ervin. I want to thank you for appearing before the committee and for your testimony, and with the understanding that you will return later at the request of the committee, you are excused at this time.

Mr. Caulfield. Yes, sir.

Senator Ervin. Thank you very much.

* * *

Actually, Dean somewhat succeeded in saving himself when some three months later, he decided to head to the prosecutors "giving up" everyone around him, including the president of the United States, while offering them every purported foible (and document) that was connected directly or indirectly to generic Watergate. All of this was in order to get his subsequent deal, which turned out to be a good one for him. The D.C. legal profession was resultantly exposed to newfound clients—the likes and numbers of which has never been seen before or since.

In the transcript of the famed, March 21, 1973, "Cancer on the Presidency" White House tape, Dean deceived the president when he reported that McCord initiated the so-called commutation subject: "Uh, McCord did ask to meet with somebody and it was Jack Caulfield"—(uh, uh, John! . . . YOU initiated that specific commutation subject with McCord via a telephone call to me, which I took in the presence of a close friend at the San Clemente White House on January 6, 1973; see if your vaunted memory can bring that up). Dean continued: ". . . and he wanted to know, well, you know (coughs)—he wanted to talk about commutation and things like that."

So, that was the type of sophisticated evasion of the facts in which Dean was engaged at that late moment; further, what is now retrospectively clear is that both Dean and McCord were, in fact, the historical catalysts that initiated a rapidly descending "funnel cloud" (a.k.a. Watergate) and sent it heading directly for the White House.

Many of my White House colleagues subsequently went to jail for generically related, Watergate political activities (profoundly regrettable to me because most all of them are/were basically good and outstandingly able men, caught in a senseless political maelstrom, that none could have even remotely imagined). I did not—for two reasons, as I now see it: first, I tend to agree with Dean's candid assessment of me to Richard Nixon: "He is an incredibly cautious person," and I saw and fortuitously avoided many of the snares in the ever-hazardous trail that was the Nixon White House. My extensive BOSSI experience had served me well in that environment.

Second, Irish luck—which is the only way to describe what I later learned was a strong positive comment made about me by Judge John Sirica to the Watergate prosecutors immediately following my Watergate Committee testimony on live television. Included, was my reading of a twenty-seven-page statement in which I referred to the numerous NYPD commendations I had received for anti-terrorist work.

John Sirica, I subsequently learned, loved NY cops and, apparently, any and all of Sirica's comments were of intense interest to the politically adept Watergate prosecutors . . . (after all, there was a group of very "heavy hitters" to be tried!). Resultantly (I believe), his positive comment diminished any potential prosecutorial interest in me, a "small fry," if you will. Of course, we may never know if my observation is accurate—which is a nice way of saying I know more than I am writing here.

To back up a bit, a few months prior to Watergate, I left the White House after seeking and getting, via the President's support, the dream U. S. Department of Treasury position, Assistant Director: Criminal Enforcement—Alcohol, Tobacco, and Firearms. It was the start of a second promising career, and I enjoyed a terrific first year there with big plans underway to remake the moribund "revenuer" agency, containing over 1,500 Federal agents, into a first-class Federal law enforcement entity with a sharp focus on the firearms/explosives end of what was then a dawning (and disturbing) political terrorist trend. Additionally, I felt certain, based on my one-of-a-kind White House experience and connections, that I could provide the agency with the same Washington clout as enjoyed by the U.S. Secret Service.

But it was over in a New-York minute when McCord decided in March 1973 (nine months after his arrest), to save himself from major (Sirica threatened) jail time by publicly turning on campaign committee associates and others. In that process, he caused the Watergate case under Sirica and other judges to cascade into a plethora of prosecutions, ruined reputations, and lost jobs, which included my prized ATF position, a casualty of the above alluded-to Dean/McCord message. An additional casualty was my health, which included the onset of latent alcoholism, a heart attack, and other problems, as the madness that was Watergate drove the nation's media into excesses of every type. Everyone (including friends and relatives) even remotely connected to Watergate in 1973 was fair game—personal rights, reputations, and family privacy meant absolutely nothing.

McCord was a self-described and promoted "physical security expert" bearing former CIA credentials. I had personally interviewed and hired him in January 1972 (before I left the White House) for strict, solely defensive security work at the Republican National Committee and the Committee to Re-Elect the President (CREEP). He had been highly recommended to me for that job by a Secret Service supervisor, who had been a career associate of his. Actually, at that time I thought he was a good find.

Prior to Watergate, we were on good but reserved terms. Notwithstanding my total shock at his arrest, I had even obliquely expressed personal concerns to him for his plight. However, putting it all together much later, it became clear to me that the "expert" was at best a political amateur, with questionable judgment and likely over-sold electronic skills. Right along with him was his (also former-CIA) co-conspirator, E. Howard Hunt, who wound up essentially cowering (Dean said blackmailing) the White House via its cover-up players for very big bucks.

Speaking To Nixon about the Senior Staff not going with my submitted "Sandwedge" intelligence plan, Dean inadvertently said it all for me: ". . . uh, in retrospect—that might have been a bad call—'cause he (Caulfield) is an incredibly cautious person and—and, wouldn't have put the situation to where it is today."

Via the colossal understatement ("might have been a bad call"), Dean was, in substance, telling the President that the Senior Staff's dismissive turn-down of my hard-nosed, but realistic, 1971 campaign intelligence plan (Operation Sandwedge) was an error. I go a lot further and say that that error was, in fact, the most monumental of the Nixon Presidency in that it rapidly created the catastrophic path leading directly to the Watergate complex—and the President's eventual resignation.

In that same genesis description, Dean told Nixon that Haldeman had directed him to put together, in the fall of 1971, an intelligence plan for the upcoming 1972 campaign and that since he had no experience in such matters, he tasked me, then a member of his staff, with the preparation of a final draft document. Operation Sandwedge was a twelve-page analysis and proposal of what would be required for structuring an accurate, intelligence-assessment capability of not only the Democratic party's opposition's tactics, but also to ensure that the then powerful anti-war movement did not destroy Nixon's public campaign, as had been done to Hubert Humphrey in 1968. It also anticipated facing a Democratic campaign effort that would utilize the astute services of a leading private investigative entity called Intertel, then headed by former officials of Bobby Kennedy's Justice Department. Intertel represented, in my opinion, the potential for both formidable and sophisticated intelligence opposition tactics in that upcoming election campaign.

I had also credibly learned (from a loose-tongued participant) some of the details of a very discreet, politically adept take-no-prisoners Democratic intelligence entity that had been ad-hoc formed, based in NYC, and employed against Nixon during the 1968 campaign.

Sandwedge proposed to respond in kind during the 1972 campaign by creating a Republican Intertel, if you will. To say the least, the Presidential stakes in that game were exceptionally high. Prior experience and observations indicated to me that close U.S. elections were often won or lost solely on the quality of a candidate's intelligence capability.

I was later informed that because Mitchell wanted a lawyer for the campaign intelligence job, my plan and participation were arbitrarily scrapped and G. Gordon Liddy was resultantly hired by three members of the White House and Nixon Presidential Campaign staffs (Dean, Krogh, and McGruder). Liddy was told by Dean to not only come up with an alternate plan, but he was also given my complete Sandwedge plan, with the comment by Dean that it was deemed "inadequate." Not one of them (including Liddy) had ever been previously involved in a Presidential campaign at a staff level—from a security/intelligence perspective or otherwise.

In breaking that news to me, Dean asked for my assessment regarding Liddy's upcoming role. I gave him a suppressed Irish temper response that, I suspect, he has pondered many times since. I said, "John, you goddamn well better have him closely supervised," and I walked out of his office.

I was unaware that that moment was the opening curtain of the Shakespearean tragedy called Watergate; however, I was aware that the famous Henry Ford observation, "Experience is the thing of supreme value in life," meant absolutely nothing, in this case, to the president's senior staff decision makers.

I knew Gordon Liddy and had enjoyed his company at a few social functions in and around Washington; and, in bar talk conversations, had listened to his humorous descriptions of Black Bag jobs (breaking and entering for intelligence purposes) and other exploits occurring when he was an FBI agent. No question he was also highly intelligent. In my view, he would have made a great NYPD detective squad commander—especially in the "Fort Apache" precinct in the South Bronx—but, God help us, not the commander of a singularly inept, quasi, over the hill CIA/Cuban soldier of fortune group, which was to be not only silently sanctioned by the White House but embarrassingly paid for by the Committee to Re-Elect the President!

It's difficult, even today, not to shake my head at the asinine nature of that entire development—for not one responsible White House or presidential campaign official ever questioned or checked the credentials of the so-called Hunt "Latin team" regarding their backgrounds, motivations, intelligence bona fides, and Cuban revolutionary track record before they began acting illegally (and assertively) on behalf of the president of the United States. I spent an entire detective career in that very unique, investigative area and would have known better than anyone in the forthcoming Nixon campaign the would-be political hazards/improprieties of such an ill-advised recruitment of intelligence personnel (who were to be mindlessly directed at the most questionable of all presidential political targets—the offices of the Democratic National Committee). Therein, in a nutshell, lays the great strategic error of the Watergate catastrophe.

Thus in April 1972, a partial $250,000 sign-off on Liddy's near-insane alternate "Gemstone" plan, which unbelievably envisioned strategies for kidnapping anti-war political dissidents, sexual blackmail, wiretapping, bugging, etc. (it was presented in its entirety in the Office of the Attorney General of the United States) and was approved in a blind-leading-the-blind manner. The plan's subsequent oversight was then delegated without discussion/evaluation to twenty-five- and thirty-year-olds, who, while otherwise able members of the White House and campaign staffs were totally lacking in the necessary experience and knowledge of an intelligence gathering process for a presidential campaign. Resultantly, even today (thirty years later) historians, writers, living staff, direct participants, etc., can't/won't agree regarding who actually financed, approved, directed, and monitored the various wiretapping/bugging decisions at the Watergate complex; and, more importantly, why.

What we do accurately know is that within just forty-eight days of the approval of "Gemstone," Liddy and Hunt's ragtag team were arrested on June 17, 1972 in the DNC offices of the Watergate complex—thus, the end of the Nixon Presidency had begun.

I, therefore, unequivocally contend that had there been Sandwedge, there would have been no Liddy, no Hunt, no McCord, no Cubans, and, critically, since I, while still on the White House staff, had personally decided to negate a developing intelligence interest by Dean in the Watergate's Democratic National Committee offices seven months prior to the break-in! NO WATERGATE! Indeed, when John Mitchell called (just prior to his death) and candidly asked me why I had personally finessed and subsequently negated Dean's fledgling DNC interest at that time, I responded, "It was too dangerous, John." His long silent, non-response was quite profound. Dean, then, perhaps was right about my being an "incredibly cautious person."

To the reader of my efforts in this book, permit me to end on a philosophical and emotional note.

First, in being forced to look back on my life and law enforcement career, I can say that it has been an unusual experience. I do consider my work and the numerous commendations I received for my twenty years, in what I believe is the greatest police department in the world, the New York City Police Department, as both honorable and rewarding. It is enough that my outstanding family members are aware of that, and know that they can be proud of my NYPD Patrolman and Detective service, in the very special area of police work, I had chosen as a career.

As the reader, you can see that my White House experience is also cherished. Very few people have the opportunity to serve the President of the United States, in that special of all places, the White House. Those that do know full well the sacrifice and effort that goes into supporting their president during their precious time at that most sacred office in our land.

To my great personal regret, I am still deeply saddened by the events that led to the tragic resignation of a man I admired, Richard Milhous Nixon. He certainly had his faults but, candidly, I have many more than him and will always respect his intellect and the incredible dilemma he was confronted with as the madness that was Watergate unraveled before him.

In my personal error of trying to assist him in the waning moments of the Watergate cover-up, I can only say two things: (a) I was wrong in consenting to pass on a clemency message to James McCord, and (b) I am deeply grateful for the fact that my testimony was not necessary for the court proceedings, which ensued at the various Watergate trials and civil suits that followed.

Personal loyalty to the President was and is, I suggest, the most precious character trait that I have been blessed with. In the end, with the help of my God, and lots of prayers, it came out okay for me, in that I was spared the further pain of incarceration and was not responsible for any of my colleagues, friend or not, experiencing that most tragic of experiences.

I leave you with this final thought. I have decided to decline ANY personal remuneration for this written effort. ALL proceeds from the e-book and/or hard copy will go not to me personally but to the foundation I have set up for the still-suffering families of the NYPDF/FDNY members who gave the ultimate sacrifice on 9/11. It has been appropriately named, "The Shield 911 Foundation Inc." Currently, any donations beyond the purchase of the book can, if you choose, be sent to my current address, 534 7th Place, Vero Beach, 32962 in that Foundation name. Please indicate

"In care of John J. Caulfield" on the envelope. I will respond with a note and a signed photograph.

I thank you all. I can be reached via US mail at: "The Shield #911-NYPD Foundation Inc." P.O. Box 651141, Vero Beach, Florida.

God Bless you and yours,
Jack Caulfield
July 15, 2008

About the Author

John "Jack" Caulfield worked as a New York City Police Department detective in the unit charged with guarding heads of state. He joined the White House staff from 1969 to 1972 and testified before the Senate Watergate Committee on Capitol Hill. Now retired, Caulfield lives in Vero Beach, Florida.